The Jesus Controversy

THE ROCKWELL LECTURE SERIES
GERALD P. McKENNY, GENERAL EDITOR

The Rockwell Lectures constitute the oldest designated and now endowed lecture series at Rice University, Houston, Texas. Since 1938, when the inaugural lecture was delivered, the Rockwell Fund has generously supported the series. The lectures are dedicated to the general subject of religion.

In the series:

Beyond Liberalism and Fundamentalism
Nancey Murphy

Christianity and Civil Society
Robert Wuthnow

The Jesus Controversy
John Dominic Crossan, Luke Timothy Johnson, and Werner H. Kelber

THE JESUS CONTROVERSY

Perspectives in Conflict

John Dominic Crossan
Luke Timothy Johnson
Werner H. Kelber

TRINITY PRESS
INTERNATIONAL
HARRISBURG, PENNSYLVANIA

Trinity Press International, P.O. Box 1321, Harrisburg, PA 17105
Trinity Press International is a division of the Morehouse Group.

Library of Congress Cataloging-in-Publication Data

Crossan, John Dominic.
   The Jesus controversy : perspectives in conflict / John Dominic
Crossan, Luke Timothy Johnson, Werner H. Kelber.
     p. cm.—(The Rockwell lecture series)
   Includes bibliographical references and index.
   ISBN 1-56338-289-X (alk. paper)
   1. Jesus Christ—Historicity. I. Johnson, Luke Timothy.   II. Kelber,
Werner H.   III. Title.   IV. Series: Rockwell lecture series (Valley Forge, Pa.)
BT303.2.C75   1999
232.9'08—dc21   99-16448
                                              CIP

Printed in the United States of America

00 01 02 03 04   6 5 4 3 2

Contents

1

Historical Jesus as Risen Lord

John Dominic Crossan

I begin with two preliminary points, one negative, one positive. First, it is important to emphasize clearly what my argument does *not* propose. It does not propose that history equals faith. It does not propose that history replaces faith. It does not propose that history creates faith. If two individuals saw and heard everything that the historical Jesus said and did in the first century, they could still respond like this. The one: he is a subversion of the Roman gods of law and order, he is dangerous and criminal, he should be executed. The other: he is an incarnation of the Jewish God of justice and righteousness, he is Messiah and Lord, he should be worshiped. The same applies to us today if we had a complete videotape of all that data. It would not be faith. It would not force faith. It would not guarantee faith. In other words, there can be history without faith. But, and this is the question, *can* there be *faith without history?* If faith is not in the discernible facts, but in the ultimate meanings of history, what sort of Christian faith could exist without historical reconstruction? In summary, the question is not: could there be research on the historical Jesus without faith in the risen Jesus? The answer to that is easy: of course there could, in the first century, in the twentieth century, and in all the centuries in between. The question is, could there be faith in the risen Jesus without research on the historical Jesus? And that is not an easy question.

Second, against that negative background, my argument can be stated through degrees of ever-more-precise focus. It is about history and faith. It is about historical reconstruction and Christian faith. It is about historical reconstruction and

1

Christian faith but within one type rather than another type of Christianity. It is about the scholarly reconstruction of the historical Jesus and religious faith in the risen Lord, but within what I will later describe as sarcophilic and/or incarnational rather than sarcophobic and/or docetic Christianity. The core questions are these. One: what is the necessary relationship, *within that former type of Christianity*, between the flesh-and-blood body of the historical Jesus and the flesh-and-blood-body of the risen Lord? Another: if, as I argue, the fleshly, bloodly, bodily resurrection of Jesus is absolutely necessary in that former type of Christianity, what is meant by that claim?

PREAMBLE ON HISTORY

There is an oft-repeated and rather cheap gibe that historical Jesus researchers are simply looking down a deep well and seeing their own reflections from below. I call it cheap because those who use it against others seldom apply it to themselves. It was cheap at the start of this century when George Tyrell, Irish and Catholic, said about Adolf von Harnack, German and Protestant, that the Christ he saw looking back through nineteen centuries of Catholic darkness is only the reflection of a liberal Protestant face seen at the bottom of a deep well.[1] It is still cheap at the end of this century when a scholar asserts that someone like myself looks down a deep well and sees there an Irish-Catholic peasant. That scholar, by the way, is herself a British Anglican theologian. There is irony as well as water in that well.

A well, however, is a good metaphor for thinking about one's theory of history. Imagine two alternative and opposite modes of historical reconstruction, one an impossible delusion, the other a possible illusion. The possible illusion is *narcissism* or *historical solipsism*. You think you are seeing the past or the other when all you see is your own reflected present. You see only what you yourself have brought with you. You imprint your own present on the past and call it history. Narcissism or solipsism sees its own face and, ignoring the water that shows it up, falls in love with itself.

The impossible delusion is *historicism* or *historical positivism*. It imagines that you can know the past without any interference from your own personal and social situation as knower. You can see, as it were, without your own eye being involved. You can discern the past, once and for all forever, and see it pure and uncontaminated by that discernment. Positivism or historicism is the

---

1. George Tyrell, *Christianity at the Crossroads* (London: George Allen and Unwin, 1963), 49.

delusion that we can see the water without our own face being mirrored in it. It thinks we can see the surface without simultaneously seeing our own eyes.

There is, therefore, a third alternative, and I will call it *interactivism* or *historical dialectic*. The past and present must interact with one another, each changing and challenging the other. The ideal is an absolutely fair and equal reaction between one another. Back to the well. You cannot see the surface without simultaneously seeing, disturbing, and distorting your own face. You cannot see your own face without simultaneously seeing, disturbing, and distorting the surface. That is the historical dialectic of interactivism and, as distinct from either narcissism or positivism, it is both possible and necessary. And, if and when you succeed in seeing your own face at the bottom of a deep well, it will look strangely different from that in your everyday mirror.

This, then, is my working definition of history: *History is the past reconstructed interactively by the present through argued evidence in public discourse.* There are times we can only get alternative perspectives on the same event. And there are always alternative perspectives even when we do not hear them. But history as argued public reconstruction is possible because it is necessary. We reconstruct our past to project our future. And it is, unfortunately, *not* possible *not* to do it. I have four corollaries to that position.

The first corollary is, of course, that none of this applies only, particularly, or especially to historical Jesus reconstruction. The well awaits *all* historical reconstruction. It awaits, for example, Caesar Augustus, Jesus' contemporary Roman emperor, just as well (sorry about that!). Ronald Mellor frames his book on Tacitus with these comments about four great reconstructions of Rome's transition from republican to imperial rule:

The greatest Roman historians of the last two centuries—Gibbon, Mommsen, Rostovzteff, and Syme—wrote with passion as they saw connections between Rome and their own times…. Edward Gibbon, a child of the French Enlightenment which affected his views of religion, was issued in Bowdlerized editions in Victorian England; Theodor Mommsen, the only professional historian to win the Nobel Prize for Literature, wrote a passionate, multi-volume *History of Rome* in which Caesar became the inevitable solution to republican Rome's dilemma as Mommsen himself yearned for a strongman to resolve the chaos of nineteenth-century Germany; Michael Rostovzteff brought his flight from revolutionary St. Petersburg to bear on his *Social and Economic History of the Roman Empire* (1926)—a glorification of the Roman municipal bourgeoisie; and Sir Ronald Syme's *The Roman Revolution*

(1939) looked at the rise of Augustus through the spectacles of a liberal who saw on his visits to Italy the names and trappings of Augustan Rome used by a new *dux*, Benito Mussolini, and wished to expose in a very Tacitean way the thuggish similarities between the two regimes.[2]

In all those cases powerful sociopersonal interactions between past and present resulted in towering achievements, works we call classical in both senses of that term. And, of course, their multiplicity serves as a corrective each on the other.

The second corollary concerns the difference between history and story. I emphasize this point because both contemporary North American culture and current scholarly exegetical discussion often speak too easily about story without distinguishing between historical narrative and fictional narrative. Here is an example from the former milieu, as cited by David Schacter:

> A young woman named Ann described how she recovered in therapy memories of terrible satanic ritual abuse at the hands of her parents, and also discovered that she harbored multiple personalities. Family videotapes and photos showed Ann, prior to therapy, as a vibrant young woman and a budding young singer.... "I don't care if it's true," asserted Ann's therapist, Douglas Sawin. "What's important to me is that I hear the child's truth, the patient's truth. That's what's important. What actually happened is irrelevant to me." Asked about the possibility that a client's report is a delusion, Sawin did not flinch: "We all live in a delusion, just more or less delusionary."[3]

That is a particularly horrible example, to be sure. It is bad enough if such abuse happened to Ann; it is worse if it happened and no redress was possible. But it is worst of all, for herself, for her family, for her society, if her therapist finds the distinction between fact and fiction, fantasy and history, of no importance whatsoever. In telling that incident from the recent "memory wars" in the United States, Schacter footnoted that "objective or 'historical truth'... becomes important when, as in Ann's case, a multimillion dollar law suit is filed against the alleged perpetrators."[4] But surely, even for therapy or especially for therapy, and apart from potential or actual lawsuits, there is a supreme difference between actual and delusional stories. And it is necessary to decide which is which. History matters. And history is possible because its absence is intolerable.

---

2. Ronald Mellor, *Tacitus* (New York: Routledge, 1993), 45, 164.

3. David L. Schacter, *Searching for Memory: The Brain, the Mind, and the Past* (New York: Basic Books, 1996), 262–63.

4. Ibid., 344 n. 28.

History is not the same as story. *Even if all history is story, not all story is history.* In the courtroom, for example, with a man accused of double murder, the defense and the prosecution tell very different stories. In one he is a murderer who must be condemned. In the other he is an innocent who has been framed. They are both highly competent and very entertaining storytellers but only one of those two stories is history. The other is mistake, fiction, invention, lie. At the end, when the man walks out of the courtroom, he is either a freed murderer or a framed innocent. He cannot be both. Maybe we will never know for sure *which* version is history-story and which just story-story. But we know that only one version *is* correct. And our decency, morality, and humanity demand that we never say it is all relative, perspective, hype, and spin, or that, since we cannot know for sure, it does not matter at all.

The third corollary concerns the term *search* or *quest*. I do not speak of the *search* for the historical Jesus or of the *quest* for Christian origins. Those terms seem to indicate a positivistic process in which we are going to attain an answer once and for all forever. That is not how I now imagine the process. I speak instead of *reconstruction*, and that is something that must be done over and over again in different times and different places, by different groups and different communities, and by every generation again and again and again. The reason, of course, is that historical reconstruction is always interactive of present and past. Even our *best* theories and methods are still *our* best ones. They are all dated and doomed not just when they are wrong but especially when they are right. They need, when anything important is involved, to be done over and over again. That does not make history worthless. We ourselves are also dated and doomed, but that does not make life worthless. It just makes death inevitable.

The final corollary concerns method. I insist that Jesus-reconstruction, like all such reconstruction, is always a creative interaction of past and present. But what keeps that dialectic of us and them as even and honest as possible? Method, method, and, once again, method. It will not guarantee us the truth because nothing can do that. But method, as self-conscious and self-critical as we can make it, is our only discipline. It cannot ever take us out of our present skins and bodies, minds and hearts, societies and cultures. But it is our one best hope for honesty. It is the due process of history.

APPARITIONS AFFIRMED, APPARITIONS NEGATED

Asked about the birth of Christianity, most people might say something like this. His followers thought Jesus was the Messiah and/or the Son of God, but then he was officially tortured and legally executed by Roman imperial power.

Within three days, however, his tomb was found empty and he appeared to his former companions as risen from the dead. Those resurrectional visions explain the miracle of Christianity's birth and growth, spread and triumph, across the Roman empire. I raise two questions about that explanation and especially about its emphasis on visions or apparitions. First, is that the way his first followers understood such visions or apparitions? If it is, how do we explain the strong affirmation of those visions in Paul *as compared with* their equally strong negation in Mark? Second, is that the way first-century people argued the significance of such visions or apparitions? Would they argue that risen visions of Jesus were unique in all the world?

One preliminary comment about terminology. I use *vision* and *apparition* interchangeably, and I understand them within the psychosocial and cross-cultural anthropology of comparative religion in works such as those by Ioan Lewis, Erika Bourguignon, Felicitas Goodman, or Raymond Prince.[5] It is imperative, against that background, to distinguish between vision or apparition and delusion or hallucination. It is helpful, in making that distinction, to compare dreams and visions. Hopes and fears, dreams and nightmares, visions and apparitions are not the same as delusions and hallucinations. If a man wakes up screaming because a giant figure is ready to attack him, that is a nightmarish dream. His wife says, "It's just a bad dream, go back to sleep." And he does. But if he calls 911 that night to report an intruder and ADT the next day to put in a security system, he is moving from dream into delusion. It is part of reality to know which is which. If that man came down from the mountaintop and reported a revelation from the Archangel Michael, he had an apparition. If he kept insisting that there was a Bigfoot-with-Wings up there and everyone should go up to see it, he would be beyond vision and into hallucination. It is part of reality to know which is which. The present discussion is not about delusions and hallucinations, about losing touch with reality, and neither is it about tricks and lies, about losing touch with honesty. Trance and ecstasy, vision and apparition are perfectly normal and natural phenomena.

---

5. Ioan M. Lewis, *Ecstatic Religion: An Anthropological Study of Spirit Possession and Shamanism*, Pelican Anthropology Library (Baltimore: Penguin, 1971); Erika Bourguignon, *A Cross-Cultural Study of Dissociational States: Final Report* (Columbus: Ohio University Press, 1968); Bourguignon, *Psychological Anthropology: An Introduction to Human Nature and Cultural Differences* (New York: Holt, Rinehart and Winston, 1979); Bourguignon, ed., *Religion, Altered States of Consciousness, and Social Change* (Columbus: Ohio University Press, 1973); Felicitas D. Goodman, *Ecstasy, Ritual, and Alternate Reality: Religion in a Pluralistic World* (Bloomington: Indiana University Press, 1988); Raymond Prince, ed., *Trance and Possession States* (Montreal: R. M. Bucke Memorial Society, 1968).

They are not, strictly speaking, even supernatural or paranormal. Altered states of consciousness, such as dreams and visions, are possibilities common to our humanity, possibilities hard-wired into our brains, possibilities as normal as language itself. They were recognized as common possibilities in the early first century, and they are still recognized as such in the late twentieth century. And only when their human normalcy is accepted can a proper response be offered. It should not be this: We deny the *fact* of your vision. It should be this: Tell us the *content* of your vision. And then we will have to judge not whether he had it or not, but whether we should follow it or not.

The problem I begin with concerns two very early accounts of the resurrectional apparitions of Jesus and, specifically, with their detailed affirmation in Paul and their total omission in Mark. What do we learn from that difference about the proposed universal significance of those visions for the birth of Christianity?

Burial and Apparition in Paul

Twenty years after the execution of Jesus, Paul recalled to his Corinthian converts the tradition that he had received and had already handed on to them. I give it in linear format to emphasize how much space and detail are given to the list of apparitions in 1 Cor. 15:1–11. The burial is mentioned almost in passing, but the risen visions are given in very great detail:

Now I would remind you, brothers and sisters, of the good news that I proclaimed to you, which you in turn received, in which also you stand, through which also you are being saved, if you hold firmly to the message that I *proclaimed* to you—unless you have come to *believe* in vain. For I handed on to you as of first importance what I in turn had received:
    that Christ died for our sins in accordance with the
    scriptures,
        and that he was buried,
    and that he was raised on the third day in accordance with the
    scriptures,
        and that he appeared
    (1) to Cephas,
    (2) then to the twelve.
    (3) Then he appeared to more than five hundred brothers and sisters
    at one time, most of whom are still alive, though some have died.
    (4) Then he appeared to James,

(5) then to all the apostles.

(6) Last of all, as to one untimely born, he appeared also to me. For I am the least of the apostles, unfit to be called an apostle, because I persecuted the church of God. But by the grace of God I am what I am, and his grace toward me has not been in vain. On the contrary, I worked harder than any of them—though it was not I, but the grace of God that is with me.

Whether then it was I or they, so we *proclaim* and so you have come to *believe*.

The whole unit is framed between the terms *proclaim/believe* in 15:1 and 11, but it is obvious that Christ's appearance to Paul himself in 15:8–11 was not part of his received tradition. One must also allow for some redactional organization whereby Paul concludes with "all the apostles" in 15:7b in order to prepare for himself as "least of the apostles" in 15:9. But, granted that, 15:3b–7 is certified as tradition *received* by Paul (15:3a) and thence *received* by the Corinthians (15:1b). But in that *received* summary slightly more space is given to the list of apparitions than to the presumably more important death and resurrection "according to the scriptures." One could fairly conclude from 1 Cor. 15:3b–7 that those apparitions or visions are profoundly important for traditional Christian faith. Twenty years later, however, Mark wrote a gospel where Jesus' death and resurrection were certainly "according to the scriptures" but where apparitions or visions were completely absent. I look at the ending of Mark's narrative gospel, in comparison with the ending of Paul's credal summary, to see what was and was not negotiable about those apparitions. Why, negatively, does Mark end without any apparitions of the resurrected Jesus? Why, positively, does Mark end as it does? How much of this is historical accuracy, traditional piety, or Markan creativity?

Burial and Apparition in Mark

Writing twenty years or so after the execution, Paul recalled, as just seen, the tradition he had received about death, burial, resurrection, and multiple apparitions. Writing about twenty years or so after Paul, Mark told that story in a very different way. There is now much more detail about the burial and tomb of Jesus but risen apparitions are totally absent. Instead of resurrectional vision we have an empty tomb. I look, moving backwards in Mark, first at the finding of Jesus' empty tomb and then at the account of Jesus' burial.

The Tomb of Jesus

Five gospels agree that Mary Magdalene and some other women are the *first* of Jesus' companions to find his tomb empty. Mark 16:1 mentions "Mary Magdalene, and Mary the mother of James, and Salome." Matt. 28:1 has "Mary Magdalene and the other Mary." Luke 24:1 cites "Mary Magdalene, Joanna, Mary the mother of James, and the other women with them." John 20:1 has only "Mary Magdalene," although she uses "we" in 20:2. *The Gospel of Peter* 12:50–51 speaks of "Mary Magdalene, a woman disciple of the Lord… [who] took with her women friends." That is a very impressive consensus, but it is all dependent on a single source. It is not five independent witnesses. It is four other writers copying directly or indirectly from Mark. It does not help to speak of "all four Gospels and… even… the *Gospel of Peter*" or of "all four Gospels" or of "the triple tradition" of Matthew, Mark, and Luke, as Claudia Setzer does.[6] That is simply counting versions while ignoring sources. The question is: do we have one, two, three, four, or five *independent* sources? And, if we only have one independent source in Mark, it all comes down to this: is there any pre-Markan tradition in Mark 16:1–8 and what is Mark's purpose for that incident? There are three linked texts to be considered:

> Mark 15:40–41 (*after the death*): There were also women looking on from a distance; among them were Mary Magdalene, and Mary the mother of James the younger and of Joses, and Salome. These used to follow him and provided for him when he was in Galilee; and there were many other women who had come up with him to Jerusalem.

> Mark 15:47 (*after the burial*): Mary Magdalene and Mary the mother of Joses saw where the body was laid.

> Mark 16:1–8 (*after the Sabbath*): When the sabbath was over, Mary Magdalene, and Mary the mother of James, and Salome bought spices, so that they might go and anoint him. And very early on the first day of the week, when the sun had risen, they went to the tomb. They had been saying to one another, "Who will roll away the stone for us from the entrance to the tomb?" When they looked up, they saw that the stone, which was very large, had already been rolled back. As they entered the tomb, they saw a young man, dressed in a white robe, sitting on the right

---

6. Claudia Setzer, *Jewish Responses to Early Christians: History and Polemics, 30–150 C.E.* (Minneapolis: Fortress Press, 1994), 160, 261, 268.

side; and they were alarmed. But he said to them, "Do not be alarmed; you are looking for Jesus of Nazareth, who was crucified. He has been raised; he is not here. Look, there is the place they laid him. But go, tell his disciples and Peter that he is going ahead of you to Galilee; there you will see him, just as he told you." So they went out and fled from the tomb, for terror and amazement had seized them; and they said nothing to anyone, for they were afraid.

That reaction could be explained as numinous awe, but it is also a rather negative portrayal of the women. It is also self-contradictory. If they told no one, how did Mark, unless "he" was one of them, know about it? But it all fits quite exactly as a conclusion to Mark's gospel.

Mark is severely and relentlessly critical of the Twelve in general, of Peter, James, and John in particular, and of Peter above all the others. That has been interpreted as Markan criticism of other Christian communities who are less emphatic about the suffering destiny of Jesus, less enthusiastic about the mission to the pagans, and more dependent on traditions about Peter, the Three, and the Twelve for their theological viewpoints. It has also been interpreted as Markan consolation for those in his own community who have failed Jesus in recent persecutions attendant on the First Roman War of 66–73/74 C.E. and who need to be told that, as with Peter, the Three, and the Twelve, failure, flight, and even denial are not hopeless. But, against that background, how could Mark end his gospel with apparitions to Peter, or the Inner Three, or the Twelve? He had to end his gospel very differently. Mark's ending in 16:1–8 must be understood against that general background and within this specific foreground:

(A[1]) Failure over crucifixion (named male disciples): Mark 10:32–42 (Gethsemane)

(B[2]) Success over resurrection (unnamed female disciple): Mark 14:3–9 (anointing)

(A[2]) Success over crucifixion (unnamed male disciple): Mark 15:39 (centurion)

(B[1]) Failure over resurrection (named female disciples): Mark 16:1–8 (empty tomb)

All of that structure is important to understand Mark's purpose. Female and male companions of Jesus are important for Mark, and the Inner Three from each group are especially important for him. But they are important as models of failure, not of hopeless failure, but still of failure. That explains why Mark created the empty tomb story just as he created the sleeping disciples in Gethsemane. The outer frames of the passion story in 10:32–42 and 16:1–8 have male and female disciples failing Jesus. But each of those twin failures is counterpointed with a twin success. Male disciples flee Jesus because they fear the crucifixion, but the centurion confesses him because he sees the crucifixion. Female disciples fail Jesus because of anointing, but another female succeeds precisely there. That needs further explanation.

In Mark's story Jesus had told the disciple three times and very clearly that he would be executed in Jerusalem and that he would rise after three days. That prophecy is repeated in 8:31, in 9:31, and in 10:33–34. It always concludes with the resurrection "after three days rise." Bringing burial spices to Jesus' tomb after those prophecies is certainly an act of love but hardly an act of faith. It is, for Mark, a lack of faith. That, rather than flight or silence, is what makes 16:1–8 failure for Mark. It is not that they flee the tomb with fear, but that they approach the tomb with ointment. That is why Mark insists that the women "bought spices, so that they might go and anoint him." But before Mark tells of that failure by named women in 16:1–8, he tells this story of stunning faith in 14:3–9:

> While he was at Bethany in the house of Simon the leper, as he sat at the table, a woman came with an alabaster jar of very costly ointment of nard, and she broke open the jar and poured the ointment on his head. But some were there who said to one another in anger, "Why was the ointment wasted in this way? For this ointment could have been sold for more than three hundred denarii, and the money given to the poor." And they scolded her. But Jesus said, "Let her alone; why do you trouble her? She has performed a good service for me. For you always have the poor with you, and you can show kindness to them whenever you wish; but you will not always have me. She has done what she could; she has anointed my body beforehand for its burial. Truly I tell you, wherever the good news is proclaimed in the whole world, what she has done will be told in remembrance of her."

This unnamed woman believes those prophecies of his death and resurrection given by Jesus in Mark 8:31, 9:31, and 10:33–34. She *believes* them and knows, therefore, that if she does not anoint him for burial now she will never be able to do it later. That is why she gets that astonishing statement of praise, one unparalleled in the entire gospel: "wherever the good news is proclaimed in the whole world, what she has done will be told in remembrance of her." That accolade is given because, in Mark's gospel, this is the first complete and unequivocal act of faith in Jesus' suffering and rising destiny. It is the only such full act before that of the equally unnamed centurion beneath the cross in 15:39b: "Truly this man was God's Son!" For Mark, that unnamed woman is the first Christian.

The empty tomb story is neither an early historical event nor a late legendary narrative but a deliberate Markan creation. Sleeping male disciples in the garden and anointing women disciples at the tomb are Mark's own redactional frames for the passion-resurrection story. It is not in 16:1–8 but in 14:3–9 that Mark portrays an "excellent woman" as a "female witness to the resurrection," to borrow Setzer's titular terms. But that is surely far more startling than to claim that a woman or women were first to find an empty tomb or even first to see the risen Jesus. Mark says a woman was first to believe in the resurrection. To someone concerned with firsts, that does seem the more significant one.

Finally, if Mark created both the burial by Joseph and the finding of the empty tomb by women, the function of 15:47 becomes clear. It is the necessary conjection between those twin units: "Mary Magdalene and Mary the mother of Joses saw where the body was laid." But those women were first introduced near the cross in 15:40–41:

> There were also women looking on from a distance; among them were Mary Magdalene, and Mary the mother of James the younger and of Joses, and Salome. These used to follow him and provided for him when he was in Galilee; and there were many other women who had come up with him to Jerusalem.

That is the fullest identification given to those three women. In Mark 15:47 neither James nor Salome is mentioned. It speaks only of "Mary Magdalene and Mary the mother of Joses." In Mark 16:1 the three women are there but Joses is not mentioned. It speaks of "Mary Magdalene, and Mary the mother of James, and Salome." It is as if Mark dismembered 15:40 to create divergently briefer versions of it in 15:47 and 16:1.

Mark knows about a group of male disciples, among whom are the Inner Three of Peter, James, and John. He criticizes them repeatedly and cumulatively. But, while that criticism is from Markan redaction, the existence and names of those men are from pre-Markan tradition. Mark also knows a group of female disciples. Just as with the men, so also with the women. Their existence and names in 15:40–41 are pre-Markan tradition, but their criticism in

15:47–16:8 is Markan redaction. In other words, the story of the women observing the burial and visiting the tomb is no earlier than Mark but the women watching the crucifixion is received tradition. But is it historical fact? My best answer is yes because the male disciples had fled and, without the women watching, we would not even know the brute fact of crucifixion as distinct, for example, from Jesus being summarily speared or beheaded in prison.

A First Objection

There are two objections to the suggestion that Mark created the empty tomb story to replace risen visions as the gospel's conclusion. One is internal and I look at it here; the other is external, and I consider it below.

The internal objection is that, in Mark 16:7, the young man in the tomb tells the women, "But go, tell his disciples and Peter that he is going ahead of you to Galilee; there you will see him, just as he told you." Does that promise apparitions and presume their later accomplishment? Are they not implicitly there in Mark just as they are explicitly there in Paul? There are four problems with that solution.

First, if Paul had ended the gospel at 16:7, that might be a persuasive reading. But he continues into this conclusion in 16:8, "So they went out and fled from the tomb, for terror and amazement had seized them; and they said nothing to anyone, for they were afraid." The message, Mark says, was never delivered. It is, for this gospel, the final and climactic act of failure from the named women to the named men.

Second, that ending was not acceptable to any of the other gospels dependent on Mark. It is possible, for example, to watch Matthew change Mark and show how it should have been done and how it must now be altered. Here is how Matthew rephrases his Markan source from disobedience to obedience:

Mark 16:8	Matt. 28:8
So they went out and fled	So they left the tomb quickly
from the tomb, for terror	with fear and great joy,
and amazement had seized them;	and ran to tell his disciples.
and they said nothing to anyone,	
for they were afraid.	

First of all, the angelic command to "go" in Mark 16:7 is glossed in Matt. 28:7 as to "go quickly" and the women's obedience is underlined by the repeated "left quickly" in 28:8. Next, each of Mark's three comments is changed into its

opposite. Instead of "fled" there is "quickly" to bring the good news. Instead
of "terror and amazement" there is "fear and great joy." Instead of "said nothing to anyone" there is, as ordered, "to tell his disciples."

But even those changes are not enough to offset Mark's terrible negativity.
So Matthew adds this completely new unit, created, in my judgment, for this
very purpose, in Matt. 28:9–10:

> Suddenly Jesus met them and said, "Greetings!" And they came to him,
> took hold of his feet, and worshiped him. Then Jesus said to them, "Do
> not be afraid; go and tell my brothers to go to Galilee; there they will
> see me."

On the one hand, Jesus' message in 28:10, "go and tell my brothers to go to
Galilee; there they will see me," simply summarizes the angelic message in 28:7,
"go quickly and tell his disciples, 'He has been raised from the dead, and indeed
he is going ahead of you to Galilee; there you will see him.'" On the other, their
"worship" prepares for the next unit on a Galilean mountain when the disciples
"worshiped him." In other words, that apparition to the women in 28:9–10 is a
pure Matthean composition, created to efface the Markan ending and prepare for
the apparition of Jesus to the disciples. Furthermore, the women get a message-
vision, the disciples get a mandate-vision. As Frans Neirynck concluded almost
thirty years ago, "the account of the empty tomb in Matt. xxviii [1–10] pre-
supposes no other version than that of Mark."[7] But, for my present purpose,
Matthew is a good example of how none of the other dependent gospels accepted the Markan ending as acceptably implicit risen visions.

Third, certain early copyists were so dissatisfied with the Markan ending that
they appended more appropriate ones. The longer ending in Mark 16:9–20, for
example, is a list of apparitions reminiscent of but quite different from Paul's in
1 Cor. 15:5–8. Bruce Metzger reports for the Editorial Committee of the United
Bible Societies' Greek New Testament with this summary:

> Four endings of the Gospel according to Mark are current in the man-
> uscripts.... [O]n the basis of good external evidence and strong internal
> considerations it appears that the earliest ascertainable form of the
> Gospel of Mark ended with 16.8.... Three possibilities are open: (a) the
> evangelist intended to close his Gospel at this place; or (b) the Gospel

7.   Frans Neirynck, *Evangelica [I: 1966–1981]. Gospel Studies—Études d'èvangile:
Collected Essays by Frans Neirynck*, ed. F. Van Segbroeck (Leuven: Leuven University
Press, 1982), 289.

was never finished; or, as seems most probable, (c) the Gospel accidentally lost its last leaf before it was multiplied by transcription.[8]

The first half of that quotation has Mark *presently* ending at 16:8, that is, without any risen apparitions, but the second half proposes that Mark *originally*
continued into a now-lost conclusion, presumably with resurrectional visions.
That last suggestion cannot be either proved or disproved and I do not find it
"most probable" for what follows in my fourth point.

Fourth, an ending at 16:8 is completely understandable and even pre-
dictable in terms of Mark's redactional theology. Mark, unlike Paul, *could not*
end with risen visions to named leaders. Mark, as seen above, relentlessly criticizes named leaders by embedding them in extremely embarrassing situations
and conversations. This involves both disciples and relatives, both men and
women. Simon is *re*named Peter in 3:16 but then *de*named back to Simon in
14:37 after sleeping during Jesus' agony in Gethsemane. The Inner Three,
Peter, James, and John, are remarkably obtuse in 8:32–33 after Jesus' first prediction of passion-resurrection in 8:27–31 and in 10:35–37 after Jesus' third
prediction of passion-resurrection in 10:32–34. And the Twelve, after twin
multiplications of loaves and fishes, once for Jews in 6:35–44 and once for
Gentiles in 8:1–9, still do not understand that one loaf is enough for all
together, enough, indeed, with a lot left over, in 8:17–21:

> Jesus said to them, "Why are you talking about having no bread? Do
> you still not perceive or understand? Are your hearts hardened? Do you
> have eyes, and fail to see? Do you have ears, and fail to hear? And do you
> not remember? When I broke the five loaves for the five thousand, how
> many baskets full of broken pieces did you collect?" They said to him,
> "Twelve." "And the seven for the four thousand, how many baskets full
> of broken pieces did you collect?" And they said to him, "Seven." Then
> he said to them, "Do you not yet understand?"

Not only his disciples but also his relatives fail Jesus dismally in 3:21, 31–35
and 6:1–6. And, as seen above, the three leading women at the tomb do not
understand any more than do the three leading men in the garden. How, after
such an unceasing catalogue of failure, could Mark conclude with risen visions
to women and men, to relatives and disciples?

---

8. Bruce M. Metzger, *A Textual Commentary on the Greek New Testament,* 2nd
ed. (New York: United Bible Societies, 1994), 102, 105 n. 7.

Furthermore, visions or apparitions are themselves problematic for Mark. I read Mark 13 against the general background of the first Jewish war against Rome in 66–74 C.E. where these prophecies of Jesus in 13:5–6 and 21–23 were fulfilled for Mark's community:

> Then Jesus began to say to them, "Beware that no one leads you astray. Many will come in my name and say, 'I am he!' and they will lead many astray.... And if anyone says to you at that time, 'Look! Here is the Messiah!' or 'Look! There he is!'—do not believe it. False messiahs and false prophets will appear and produce signs and omens, to lead astray, if possible, the elect. But be alert; I have already told you everything."

Apocalyptic consummation is still imminent for Mark, as in 9:1 where Jesus foretells that there are "some standing here who will not taste death until they see that the kingdom of God has come with power." But in between resurrection and parousia there are no resurrectional apparitions, not in the 30s and not in the 70s C.E. In between is the time of trial and suffering, the time of an absent Lord or, better, the time of a Lord present only in the community of those persecuted as he was. In between is the time not of risen vision but of empty tomb.

In that understanding of Mark's communal situation, historical location, and redactional theology, 16:8 is a most appropriate conclusion and the hypothesis of an unfinished gospel or a lost leaf is not necessary. The undelivered message is that "the disciples and Peter" should get out of Jerusalem and go to Galilee because it is there that Jesus will reappear to them, not in risen vision but in imminent parousia. But my main point is that those multiple risen apparitions so important for Paul's received tradition and personal experience were deliberately avoided and negated by Mark. Resurrectional faith was equally important for them both but resurrectional apparitions were not.

The Burial of Jesus

I have argued that Mark created the empty tomb narrative to replace any risen apparition story as the conclusion of the gospel. That raises one further question, linked to but separable from that first suggestion. Is the story of Joseph of Arimathea's burial of Jesus received tradition or Markan creation? There are two elements in that problem: first, *that* Jesus was buried; second, *how* Jesus was buried. Did Mark create one, both, or neither of those elements?

First, *that* Jesus was buried. Paul wrote in 1 Cor. 15:4 that Jesus "was buried." If that is received tradition, Mark could not have created the *that* of Jesus' burial.

If it is simply Paul's way of insisting that Jesus was truly dead (not just dead, but dead *and buried*) then it is presupposition rather than tradition. It is added by Paul to the tradition of the death just as his own revelation is added to the tradition of the apparitions. The *that* of burial arises because Roman crucifixion normally involved leaving the condemned person on the cross for carrion birds and prowling dogs to consume, as Martin Hengel explains:

> Crucifixion was aggravated further by the fact that quite often its victims were never buried. It was a stereotyped picture that the crucified victim served as food for wild beasts and birds of prey. In this way his humiliation was made complete. What it meant for a man in antiquity to be refused burial, and the dishonour which went with it, can hardly be appreciated by modern man.[9]

Crucifixion was not just about physical pain or social shame. It was, like condemnation to the arena beasts or the grilled fire, an attempt to annihilate the individual as fully and completely as possible. But we know from both textual and archaeological sources that exceptions to that ultimate fate were possible, although they also serve but to prove the rule. Jesus' contemporary Philo, the Jewish philosopher from Alexandria in Egypt, observed in his *Flaccus* 83 that decent governors sometimes had crucified criminals "taken down and given up to their relations, in order to receive the honours of sepulture" at the time of the emperor's birthday since "the sacred character of the festival ought to be regarded."[10] And Jesus' contemporary Jehochanan, the crucified skeleton from Giv'at ha-Mivtar in Jerusalem, still bears an iron nail about four and a half inches long in his right heel bone but he was honorably interred in ossuary and tomb.[11] That Jesus was buried is certainly possible and, if Paul intends "that he was buried" as received tradition, it may even be probable. But the horror is this: the major alternative to the body abandoned on the cross is the body dumped in a limed pit, as Marianne Sawicki has noted:

> The Gospel stories mention a gentle enshrouding, a magnanimous laying out, and a loving tombside vigil; but a limed pit is much more probable.

---

9. Martin Hengel, *Crucifixion in the Ancient World and the Folly of the Message of the Cross* (Philadelphia: Fortress Press, 1977), 87–88.

10. Philo, *The World of Philo*, trans. Charles Duke Yonge (Peabody, Mass.: Hendrikson, 1993), 732.

11. Joseph Zias and Eliezer Sekeles, "The Crucified Man from Giv'at ha-Mivtar: A Reappraisal," *IEJ* 35 (1985): 22–27.

Like countless others of the "disappeared," Jesus was not important enough to trouble the governor with… returning the remains to the family. Lime eats the body quickly and hygienically. Therefore we find virtually no skeletal remains of the thousands crucified outside Jerusalem in the first century…. Calvary had been a quarry in antiquity, and after executions the police dumped the bodies into any convenient hole together with some lime to cut the stench. But possibly the Sanhedrin took custody of Jesus' corpse according to the procedure recalled in Mishnah *Sanhedrin* 6:5 [a common criminal tomb], since the sentence of the court was not considered satisfied until the body decomposed [one year later].[12]

That quotation moves us from the *that* to the *how* of Jesus' burial and especially to the historicity of Mark's account about Joseph of Arimathea.

Second, then, *how* Jesus was buried? If Jesus was not kept on the cross as ultimate punishment, was dishonorable limed pit or honorable new tomb the most likely alternative? In other words, is Mark's account historical? I have argued in recent works that Mark created *both* the burial story and the empty tomb story as a linked conclusion to the gospel.[13] Gerald O'Collins and Daniel Kendall have debated that position by asking "Did Joseph of Arimathea Exist?" That is not exactly my question. I do not ask in general whether a Joseph of Arimathea existed or not. I ask in particular whether he did what Mark recorded, whether, in other words, Mark's account is history or not.

The major argument used by O'Collins and Kendall is that most or even all scholars disagree with me and accept the historicity of the Markan burial story. These are the framing sentences of their article:

Among the pioneers of form criticism, Rudolf Bultmann accepted the essential credibility of the burial narrative. He described the basic story (Mark 15.44–45, 47) as "an historical account which creates no impression of being a legend." More recently Joseph Fitzmyer wrote: "Joseph of Arimathea is otherwise unknown, but in all four Gospels he is linked

---

12. Marianne Sawicki, *Seeing the Lord: Resurrection and Early Christian Practices* (Minneapolis: Fortress Press, 1994), 180, 257.

13. See my *The Cross That Spoke: The Origins of the Passion Narrative* (San Francisco: Harper and Row, 1988), 234–48; *The Historical Jesus: The Life of a Mediterranean Jewish Peasant* (San Francisco: HarperSanFrancisco, 1991), 391–93; *Jesus: A Revolutionary Biography* (San Francisco: HarperSanFrancisco, 1994), 123–27, 152–58; *Who Killed Jesus? Exposing the Roots of Anti-Semitism in the Gospel Story of the Death of Jesus* (San Francisco: HarperSanFrancisco, 1995), 160–88.

to the burial of Jesus, clearly a historical reminiscence being used. Who would invent him?"… Unquestionably, the essential historicity of the burial story in Mark cannot be demonstrated absolutely, but at least we can conclude that Crossan has done nothing to undermine its historical credibility, which remains accepted by very many biblical scholars from Bultmann to Fitzmyer and beyond.[14]

First, a minor point, just to be accurate. Bultmann said that Mark 15:42–47 was "an historical account… *apart from…* v. 47, and vv. 44,45."[15] Second, the major point is not whether my opponents are many but whether their arguments are good. Bultmann is quite correct that Mark's burial story is not a legend but, as "an historical account," is it historical *fact* or historical *fiction*? He does not even ask that question or make that distinction. Fitzmyer mentions "all four Gospels" as if one counted present texts rather than assessed independent sources.[16] But since Matthew and Luke take their burial story from Mark and since, to be seen below, John is also here dependent on Mark, we are left with a single independent source. That does not prove Mark created the burial story but it requires more than an assertion of "clearly historical reminiscence" to prove that he did not. "Who would invent him?" Fitzmyer asks. Mark would, I reply, at least for his present narrative function. Third, my own argument does not just depend on "general positions (about the original source for the gospel passion narrative in an earlier version which, though no longer extant, is embedded in the Gospel of Peter; the tendency to historicize OT prophecies; and Mark's extraordinary creativity)" and one "specific point (Joseph of Arimathea as an 'in-between' figure)" as O'Collins and Kendall state.[17] I hold all of those positions, but my claim for the *un*historicity of Mark's burial narrative derives from much more specific argumentation and a close analysis of the burial texts themselves. Those general criticisms do not touch those arguments and I repeat them here once again but in expanded form. I begin with the text of Mark 15:42–47:

When evening had come, and since it was the day of Preparation, that is, the day before the sabbath, Joseph of Arimathea, a respected member of

---

14. Gerald O'Collins and Daniel Kendall, "Did Joseph of Arimathea Exist?" *Biblica* 75 (1994): 235–41.

15. Rudolf Bultmann, *The History of the Synoptic Tradition*, trans. John Marsh (New York: Harper and Row, 1963), 274. Emphasis mine.

16. Joseph A. Fitzmeyer, *The Gospel according to Luke*, 2 vols. (Garden City, N.Y.: Doubleday, 1981–85), 1526.

17. O'Collins and Kendall, "Did Joseph of Arimathea Exist?" 236.

the council, who was also himself waiting expectantly for the kingdom of God, went boldly to Pilate and asked for the body of Jesus. Then Pilate wondered if he were already dead; and summoning the centurion, he asked him whether he had been dead for some time. When he learned from the centurion that he was dead, he granted the body to Joseph. Then Joseph bought a linen cloth, and taking down the body, wrapped it in the linen cloth, and laid it in a tomb that had been hewn out of the rock. He then rolled a stone against the door of the tomb. Mary Magdalene and Mary the mother of Joses saw where the body was laid.

Somebody named Joseph of Arimathea *could* have buried Jesus either out of personal piety or out of communal duty.

Personal Piety

That is exemplified in *Tobit*, a fourth or third-century B.C.E. novel that is set in Assyria at the end of the eighth and start of the seventh centuries B.C.E. First, in 1:17, a pious Jew named Tobit says, "I would give my food to the hungry and my clothing to the naked; and if I saw the dead body of any of my people thrown out behind the wall of Nineveh, I would bury it." For this he forfeits all his property and almost loses his life as well. Next, in 2:2, at the Feast of Pentecost, Tobit invites "whatever poor person you may find of our people among the exiles in Nineveh, who is wholeheartedly mindful of God, and he shall eat together with me." Finally, in 2:4, he gets up from that untouched dinner to recover an unburied Jew from the market square and "laid it in one of the rooms until sunset when I might bury it." Joseph of Arimathea could have been a pious Jew like Tobit in that novel a few centuries before Jesus.

Communal Duty

That is exemplified by Jewish law in the *Mishnah*, a code of Jewish life assembled around the year 200 C.E. The fourth of its six divisions is on Damages and the fourth of Damages' ten tractates is on the *Sanhedrin*, or Supreme Court. *Sanhedrin* 6:5–6 notes that "they used not" to bury executed criminals in their ancestral tombs but kept two burial places in readiness, one for those "beheaded and strangled," the other for those "stoned or burnt." After a year in such places, "when the flesh had wasted away," their bones could be taken and reburied honorably by their families but without any public mourning.[18] *If* that was ever operational in real as distinct from ideal law, and *if* it was operational in early Roman Jerusalem, Joseph *could* have been the official whose duty it was to bury condemned bodies.

The problem with Joseph of Arimathea is not on the level of *could* but of *did*. It is not on the level of possibility but of actuality. In one's best historical reconstruction, did such a person do what Mark described? Two points convince me that Mark 15:42–47 is Mark's own creation. The first concerns who Joseph was, the second what Joseph did.

Who Joseph Was

Who was Joseph, as Mark tells it and as Matthew and Luke rewrite it? Mark 15:43 described him as "(1) a respected member of the council [*bouleutēs*], (2) who was also himself waiting expectantly for the kingdom of God." That is doubly and, I think, deliberately ambiguous.

It is ambiguous with regard to the first part: was Joseph among those who judged Jesus? In 14:55 and 15:1 Mark called those who judged Jesus "the whole council [*synedrion*]" or sanhedrin, and he said in 14:64 that "all of them condemned him as deserving death." But Joseph is described not as a member of the *synedrion*-council but as a member of the *boulē*-council. There was, of course, no such distinction in historical life. There was only one council, which was convened whenever Pilate and/or Caiaphas had need of it and which contained whomever they deemed appropriate at that given moment. Those divergent terms for the council make it impossible to be sure that Joseph was among the judges of Jesus and that is precisely its Markan purpose.

But it is equally ambiguous with regard to that second half: was Joseph among those who followed Jesus? We know from as early as 1:14 that the Kingdom of God is a crucial term for Mark. But is "looking for it" the same as accepting it, entering it, believing in it? That oblique expression, "looking for," makes it impossible to be sure that Joseph was among the followers of Jesus and that, once again, is precisely its Markan purpose.

Matthew and Luke, the first and most careful readers of Mark, see those problems and respond to Mark's calculated ambiguity. Matt. 27:57 eliminates any mention of the council and makes Joseph explicitly a follower of Jesus. He is now "a rich man from Arimathea, named Joseph, who was also a disciple of Jesus." Luke 22:66 picks up the term "*synedrion*-council" from Mark but solves the problem of Joseph the sanhedrist-disciple in 23:50–51: "there was a good

---

18. *The Mishnah*, trans. and ed. Herbert Danby (Oxford: Oxford University Press, 1950), 391.

and righteous man named Joseph, who, though a member of the council [*bouleutēs*], had not agreed to their plan and action. He came from the Jewish town of Arimathea, and he was waiting expectantly for the kingdom of God." Luke, of course, had not copied that earlier comment in Mark 14:64 that "all" of the council's judges had condemned Jesus to death.

What Joseph Did

What did Joseph do, as Mark tells it and as Matthew and Luke rewrite it? Mark 15:46 says that Joseph took Jesus' body and "laid it in a tomb that had been hewn out of the rock." That is clear enough unless the reader wonders who Joseph was and why he buried Jesus. If he acted out of either personal piety or communal duty, he would have done the same for the two other criminals crucified with Jesus. But, unless one imagines three separate tombs, they would all have been buried together in a single tomb or even in some communal tomb for criminals. How, then, could it continue into an empty tomb story? How ghastly to imagine probing among corpses to identify the missing one as that of Jesus?

Once again, Matthew and Luke see the problem and respond to it separately but emphatically. They both find the obvious solution: Joseph's tomb has to be one in which no one is buried before or with Jesus; he must be alone in that tomb. Matt. 27:60 rephrases Mark this way: Joseph took the body of Jesus "and laid it in his own new tomb, which he had hewn in the rock." Luke 23:53 rephrases Mark this way: Joseph took the body of Jesus "and laid it in a rock-hewn tomb where no one had ever been laid."

Mark's story presents the tradition with double dilemmas. One: If Joseph was in the council, he was against Jesus. If he was for Jesus, he was not in the council. Another: If Joseph buried Jesus from piety or duty, he would have done the same for the two other crucified criminals. If he did that, there could be no empty tomb sequence. None of those points is unanswerable, but together they persuade me that Mark created that burial by Joseph of Arimathea in 15:42–47. It contains no data from pre-Markan tradition but several problems for post-Markan tradition.

A Second Objection

The second but external objection to the theory that Mark created the stories of honorable burial and empty tomb to end the gospel without any apparitions to named leaders is this. Granted that Matthew and Luke are dependent on Mark for their versions of those events, but what about John? Are not the honorable burial in John 19:38–42 and the empty tomb in 20:1–13 independently present there, and how then could they have been created by Mark? That raises the problem of John's relationship to the Synoptics. If John is independent, Mark *could not* have created those stories. If John is dependent, Mark *could* have created those stories. And, obviously, that question must be decided first and then maintained as a historical presupposition. It cannot be decided in a vicious circle from one's position on Mark's alleged creation of those stories.

In debating my views, O'Collins and Kendall recognize this problem but they solve it, as usual, by an appeal to alternative authority rather than comparative argument. "As [John P.] Meier points out, 'most of the major commentators on John in recent decades' hold that John represents 'a tradition independent of the Synoptics.'"[19] If matters could be resolved simply by citation rather than argumentation, here are two scholars opposing Meier. First, Adelbert Denaux, introducing the published papers of an international meeting on John and the Synoptic Gospels at Belgium's Leuven University in 1990, claimed, maybe too strongly, that there was now "a growing consensus that the author of the Fourth Gospel was related to and/or in one way or another dependent upon one or more of the Synoptic Gospels."[20] Second, Dwight Moody Smith, after a very thorough historical review of scholarship on that relationship, summarized the present situation very accurately: "At the beginning of the century, the exegete or commentator could safely assume John's knowledge of the Synoptics. We then passed through a period of a quarter of a century or more (1955–80) in which the opposite assumption was the safer one: John was perhaps ignorant of the Synoptics, certainly independent of them. We have now reached a point at which neither assumption is safe, that is, neither can be taken for granted."[21] But, once again, it is one's argument, not one's citation, that counts, so here, in necessarily swiftest summary,[22] is my basic argument for John's dependence on the Synoptic tradition, especially in his passion-resurrection account.

One of the most peculiarly distinctive Markan compositional devices has been called an *intercalation* or *sandwich*. The device has two elements. First,

---

19. O'Collins and Kendall, "Did Joseph of Arimathea Exist?" 240–41. The citation of Meier is from *Horizons* 16 (1989): 379.

20. Adelbert Denaux, ed., *John and the Synoptics* (Leuven: Leuven University Press, 1992), viii.

21. Dwight Moody Smith, "The Problem of John and the Synoptics in the Light of the Relation between Apocryphal and Canonical Gospels," in *John and the Synoptics*, ed. Denaux, 189.

22. For a fuller account, see my *Who Killed Jesus?* 62–63, 100–105.

literary presentation: Event *A* begins (call it *A¹*), then Event *B* begins and fin-ishes (call it *B*), and finally, Event *A* finishes (call it *A²*). Second, theological meaning: the purpose of the intercalation is not mere literary show; it pre-sumes that those two events, the framing event (*A¹* + *A²*) and the insert event (*B*), are mutually interactive, that they interpret one another to emphasize Mark's theological intention. It is this combination of literary structure and theological import that makes those intercalations peculiarly if not uniquely Markan. Furthermore, there is a fairly wide agreement on the following six cases as examples of Markan intercalations:

A^1:	3:20–35	5:21–24	6:7–13	11:12–14	14:1–2	14:53–54
B:	3:22–30	5:25–34	6:14–29	11:15–19	14:3–9	14:55–65
A^2:	3:31–35	5:35–43	6:30	11:20–21	14:10–11	14:66–72

Several scholars agree on those six instances but add others as well. For example, Frans Neirynck gives seven, John Donahue also seven, and James Edwards nine examples.[23] "The Evangelist," as Tom Shepherd summarizes Mark's purpose from those six cases, "has brought two stories together and yet held them apart in contrast to one another to produce an interpretation."[24] In 14:53–72, for example, there is a supremely ironic contrast: "Jesus gives a faithful confession of his Messiahship and receives the sentence of death [in *A¹* + *A²*]. Peter denies his Lord three times and saves himself from suffering [in *B*]."[25] Those Markan inter-calations are almost as distinctive as literary fingerprints or theological DNA, and when I find them present in other gospels I recognize dependency on Mark.

Focus now on the sixth example in the above list, the one in 14:53–72 just mentioned by Shepherd. What Mark did was intercalate Jesus' confession under trial in 14:55–65 (= *B*) between the beginning in 14:53–54 (= *A¹*) and ending in 14:66–72 (= *A²*) of Peter's denials. Since Mark's community is repeatedly warned about persecution, the point of that sandwiched juxtaposi-tion is very clear. People should take Jesus as the model for brave and open confession of the truth under trial. But, if they deny Jesus under pressure and even curse him to prove their innocence, there is still hope for repentance and forgiveness—surely, a very consoling double message *about* Christians who died

---

23. Frans Neirynck, *Duality in Mark: Contributions to the Study of the Markan Redaction* (Leuven: Leuven University Press, 1972), 133; John R. Donahue, *Are You the Christ? The Trial Narrative in the Gospel of Mark* (Cambridge: SBL, 1973), 42 n. 2 and 58–59; James R. Edwards, "Markan Sandwiches: The Significance of Interpolations in Markan Narratives," *Novum Testamentum* 31 (1989): 197–98.

24. Tom Shepherd, "The Narrative Function of Markan Intercalation," *New Testament Studies* 41 (1995): 523.

25. Ibid., 532.

bravely through confession and *for* Christians who survived safely through denial.

That *A¹-B-A²* inclusion of Mark 14:53–72 is retained in Matt. 26:57–75 but eliminated in Luke 22:56–71, where Peter's denials in 22:54–62 simply precede Jesus' confession in 22:63–71. But here is the important point. John not only presents the same *A¹-B-A²* pattern but, if anything, he intensifies it by having one denial precede (18:13–18) and two others follow (18:25–27) Jesus' confession (18:19–24). His purpose was probably not just to contrast Jesus and Peter, as Mark did, but also to contrast Peter and "the other disciple" in 18:15–17:

> Simon Peter and another disciple followed Jesus. Since that disciple was known to the high priest, he went with Jesus into the courtyard of the high priest, but Peter was standing outside at the gate. So the other disciple, who was known to the high priest, went out, spoke to the woman who guarded the gate, and brought Peter in. The woman said to Peter, "You are not also one of this man's disciples, are you?" He said, "I am not."

It is significant that nothing is said about *that other disciple,* who is presumably the same as the Beloved Disciple, denying Jesus! The transference of that peculiarly or even uniquely Markan literary-theological structure from Mark 14:53–72 into John 18:13–27 persuades me to accept, at least as a working hypothesis, the dependence of John's passion-resurrection account on Mark's. Further arguments for that dependency are given by Maurits Sabbe for the passion narratives[26] and by Frans Neirynck for the resurrection narratives.[27]

John's account of Jesus' burial is, first, dependent on the Synoptics, that is, for me, dependent on a Markan creation. And it is, second, in climactic accord with John's theology of passion-as-resurrection, crucifixion-as-ascension to the Father from whence Jesus came. Joseph is a secret disciple, he is accompanied by another one, Nicodemus, and they bury Jesus with "a mixture of myrrh and aloes, weighing about a hundred pounds" in 19:39. I find there a trajectory of hope but not of history. Behind that hope lies, at worst, the horror of a body

---

26. Maurits Sabbe, "The Arrest of Jesus in Jn 18, 1–11 and Its Relation to the Synoptic Gospels: A Critical Evaluation of A. Dauer's Hypothesis," and "The Trial of Jesus before Pilate in John and Its Relation to the Synoptic Gospels," in *Studia Neotestamentica: Collected Essays* (Leuven: Leuven University Press, 1991), 355–88, 467–513; Sabbe, "The Johannine Account of the Death of Jesus and Its Synoptic Parallels (Jn 19, 16b–42)," *ETL* 70 (1994): 34–64; and Sabbe, "The Denial of Peter in the Gospel of John," *Louvain Studies* 20 (1995): 219–40.

27. Neirynck, *Evangelica I,* 181–488; *Evangelica II: 1982–1991. Collected Essays by Frans Neirynck,* ed. F. Van Segbroeck (Leuven: Leuven University Press, 1991), 571–616.

left on the cross as carrion or, at best, a body consigned like others to a "limed pit," as Sawicki put it above. I would hope for Joseph's generosity or even Nicodemus's extravagance, but what one hopes for is not always what happens.

APPARITIONS THEN, APPARITIONS NOW

The preceding section contrasted two very early Christians who believed absolutely in the resurrection of Jesus but for whom risen apparitions were, on the one hand, fully emphasized and, on the other, completely avoided. In contrast to Paul's received tradition in 1 Corinthians 15 stands Mark 15–16 which, in my view, created both the honorable burial and empty tomb precisely to avoid such resurrectional visions. I leave aside, for here and now, the equally diverse ways that Luke and John handle such phenomena. But recall, at least in passing, the warning of Luke 16:31, "If they do not listen to Moses and the prophets, neither will they be convinced even if someone rises from the dead," and of John 20:29 that "Blessed are those who have not seen and yet have come to believe." In view, then, of that contrast between Paul and Mark, I go back into that first century and *try* to see resurrectional apparitions with first-century eyes. Hear, then, the next paragraph very carefully.

It all began with the vision of a dead man, a dead man still bearing the wounds of his execution, an execution as horrible as hate could devise and contempt accomplish. And it happened outside the city walls where dogs and crows waited for an unburied body. There was also a story. It told of a community, conceived in heaven but born on earth. It told of a kingdom standing in opposition to the other kingdoms of the world. It told of an individual, peacemaker and lord, savior and son of god, who proclaimed that kingdom's advent as gospel, good news for all the earth.

I am not, however, speaking of the risen Jesus and earliest Christianity but of pagan Rome and Augustan eschatology. That story was heard as choral hymn, read as national epic, and seen as marble frieze within the Roman empire. But the inaugural vision that began the story took place over a thousand years earlier on the night the Greeks burned Troy to the ground. In Book 22 of Homer's *Iliad*, Achilles slew the Trojan hero Hector and other Greek warriors stabbed his naked corpse. Achilles had taunted the dying Hector that "the dogs and birds will maul you, shame your corpse.... [T]he dogs and birds will rend you—blood and bone." After he died, Achilles brought Hector's body back to the Greek encampment like this, in Robert Fagles's translation:

Piercing the tendons, ankle to heel behind both feet,
he knotted straps of rawhide through them both,
lashed them to his chariot, left the head to drag
and mounting the car, hoisting the famous arms aboard,
he whipped his team to a run and breakneck on they flew,
holding nothing back. And a thick cloud of dust rose up
from the man they dragged, his dark hair swirling round
that head so handsome once, all tumbled low in the dust—
since Zeus had given him over to his enemies now
to be defiled in the land of his own fathers.[28]

Only the abject pleas and supplicant humility of Hector's father, Priam, king of Troy, moved Achilles to surrender the body for honorable burial by its own people. And that is how the *Iliad* ends: with the lament of the three women closest to Hector: his wife, Andromache, his mother, Hecuba, and his sister-in-law, Helen; with funeral pyre, golden ossuary, and deep, hollow grave, and with, in its last lines, "a splendid feast in Hector's honor." But where Homer's *Iliad* ends, Virgil's *Aeneid* begins.

Julius Caesar was assassinated in March of 44 because aristocratic republicans thought he planned autocracy. Octavius, his 19-year-old adopted son and legal heir, deified Caesar in January of 42, defeated Antony and Cleopatra in September of 31, and was declared Augustus in January of 27 B.C.E. Octavius was also Peacemaker, Benefactor, Savior, and Son of a God. He was even Lord of Time itself so that his birthday on September 23 would become New Year's Day in the Roman province of Asia Minor because "the birthday of our god signalled the beginning of good news [*euaggelion*] for the world because of him." That, however, was thirty years after the crucial exchange in 27 when Octavius gave the Senate back most of the provinces and they gave Augustus back most of the legions. He now was what Caesar might have been, supreme autocrat, even if called by whatever name one chose to disguise that obvious fact. But neither deity nor power had been enough to protect Caesar from assassination. What was needed as well as the legions and power were the artists and propaganda. Virgil's *Aeneid* is superb poetry. It is also superb propaganda.

The *Aeneid* tells the story of the Roman people and especially the story of the Julian clan up to and including Caesar, Augustus, and their families. It all begins long before with the Trojan male Anchises and the Greek goddess Aphrodite. Aeneas is the human-divine or mortal-immortal child of that

---

28. Homer, *Iliad*, trans. Robert Fagles (New York: Viking, 1990), 554–55.

union and it is to him that Hector appears with the Greeks already inside the walls of the doomed city. This is that vision, from Book 2 of the *Aeneid*, in Robert Fitzgerald's translation:

> In sleep, in dream, Hector appeared to me,
> Gaunt with sorrow, streaming tears, all torn—
> As by the violent car on his death day—
> And black with bloody dust,
> His puffed-out feet cut by the rawhide thongs.
> Ah god, the look of him! How changed
> From that proud Hector who returned to Troy
> Wearing Achilles' armor, or that one
> Who pitched the torches on Danaan ships;
> His beard all filth, his hair matted with blood,
> Showing the wounds, the many wounds, received
> Outside his father's city walls.[29]

Aeneas, "child of the goddess," flees Troy, taking with him his father, Anchises, and his son, Julus. They eventually arrive in Italy and the rest is, if not exactly history, at least magnificent poetry. Virgil's great poem, unfinished at his death in 19 B.C.E. after ten years of work, celebrated "the Trojan Caesar.... Julius his name, from Julus handed down,"[30] linked heaven and earth, connected Troy and Rome, and gave the Roman people and the Augustan principate a divine origin and a mythic destiny.

Those preceding paragraphs make a very simple point. The general Mediterranean culture would find nothing impossible about that vision of Hector to Aeneas. Nothing in that story would have raised a first-century eyebrow. The dead existed in the realm of Hades or Sheol, could reappear thence to the living, and, although Hector's body had flamed to ashes on a Trojan funeral pyre, his "body" was still visible and recognizable to Aeneas. That the dead could return and interact with the living was a commonplace of the Greco-Roman world and neither pagans nor Jews would assert that it could not happen. That such interaction could generate important processes and events, as with Hector saving Aeneas to found the Roman people and the Julian ascendancy, was also commonplace. The dead were not expected to return from Hades simply to say hello. It could easily be said that such a

---

29. Virgil, *Aeneid*, trans. Robert Fitzgerald (New York: Random House, 1983), 43.
30. Ibid., 13.

return did not happen this time or that time. It could *not* be said that it never happened anywhere or could never happen at all. "The souls of the dead could certainly interact with the living and with each other, in ways exactly analogous to normal life," as Gregory Riley has shown so well.

> Instances abound in which the dead were touched and touched others.... The souls of the dead, though described as impalpable, seem not to notice this minor modification; they live and act exactly as do the living, even alongside the living.... Any Semitic or Greco-Roman soul could appear to the living, still bearing the recognizable form of the body. Any soul could pass through closed doors, give preternatural advice, and vanish. Did Jesus appear to and instruct his disciples after his crucifixion? So Patroklos appeared to Achilles, Samuel to Saul, the elder Scipio to his grandson, as did numerous others to their survivors. Did the resurrected Jesus eat broiled fish, and a meal with his disciples? Any soul could, and often did, eat with friends and relatives in the repasts of the cult of the dead, a practice perhaps especially common among Christians.[31]

An objection could *and should* be made that it is not as simple as all that. In his first letter to the Corinthians Paul explains the resurrection of Jesus as the beginning of the general resurrection at the end of the world. As a Pharisee, Paul believed in such an apocalyptic resurrection and concluded that it had *already begun* with Jesus. We often say that for Paul the end of the world was imminent. It is more accurate to say that for Paul the end had already begun and only its final consummation was imminent. That is why in 1 Cor. 15:13, 16 he can argue quite logically that Jesus' resurrection and the general resurrection stand or fall together, in 15:13, 16, 20: "If there is no resurrection of the dead, then Christ has not been raised.... For if the dead are not raised, then Christ has not been raised.... But in fact Christ has been raised from the dead, the first fruits of those who have died." It never occurs to Paul that Jesus' resurrection might be a special or unique privilege given to him because he is Messiah, Lord, and Son of God. It never occurs to Paul that Jesus' case might be like the case of Elijah, taken up individually to live with God but without any wider, communal, or cosmic effects. It is not, therefore, about the vision of a dead man but about the vision of a dead man *who begins the general resurrection*. It is an apparition with cosmically apocalyptic consequences. All of that is quite correct but it only serves to intensify the question.

---

31. Gregory John Riley, *Resurrection Reconsidered: Thomas and John in Controversy* (Minneapolis: Fortress Press, 1995), 58, 67.

Why, against that first-century background, did the vision of a resurrected Jesus make Paul and other Christians conclude that *this* was the beginning of the end and not just a personal gift for Jesus alone?

That first century not only lacked a clear separation of church and state, it also lacked a clear separation of heaven and earth. The pro-Christian defender Justin Martyr, writing his *First Apology* in the middle of the second century, and the anti-Christian attacker Celsus, writing his *On the True Doctrine* about twenty-five years later, had to agree therefore on this major point. Risen apparition and heavenly ascension were accepted possibilities of their cultural environment. Neither writer claimed that such events could not happen. Neither writer claimed that such events were unique. This is Justin's somewhat stunning assertion in his *First Apology* 21:

> And when we say also that… Jesus Christ, our Teacher, was crucified and died, and rose again, and ascended into heaven, we propound nothing different from what you believe regarding those whom you esteem sons of Jupiter. For you know how many sons your esteemed writers ascribed to Jupiter: Mercury, the interpreting word and teacher of all; Aesculapius, who, though he was a great physician, was struck by a thunderbolt, and so ascended to heaven; and Bacchus too, after he had been torn limb from limb; and Hercules, when he had committed himself to the flames to escape his toils; and the sons of Leda, and Dioscuri; and Perseus, son of Danae; and Bellerophon, who, though sprung from mortals, rose to heaven on the horse Pegasus. For what shall I say of Ariadne, and those who, like her, have been declared to be set among the stars? And what of the emperors who die among yourselves, whom you deem worthy of deification, and in whose behalf you produce some one who swears he has seen the burning Caesar rise to heaven from the funeral pyre?[32]

Christians argued, of course, that with regard to the climactic case of Jesus those pagan parallels were either created by God to prepare Christian belief or devised by Satan to confuse Christian faith. Still the argument could not be, in pro-Christian apologetics, that the case of Jesus was unique nor, in anti-Christian polemics, that such an event could not happen. Here, for example, is the best that Celsus can do to refute Christian claims about Jesus' bodily resurrection in his *On the True Doctrine*:

---

32. Justin Martyr, *First Apology*, in *The Ante-Nicene Fathers*, ed. Alexander Roberts, James Donaldson, and A. Cleveland Coxe (New York: Scribner's, 1926), 1:316–17.

Has there ever been such an incompetent planner: When he was in the body, he was disbelieved but preached to everyone; after his resurrection, apparently wanting to establish a strong faith, he chooses to show himself to one woman and a few comrades only. When he was punished, everyone saw; yet risen from the tomb, almost no one.[33]

Those are good cracks but weak criticisms. In a world where gods and goddesses, spirits and immortals, regularly interacted physically and sexually, spiritually and intellectually with human beings, the vision of a dead person is neither a totally abnormal nor a completely unique event. So, how, in terms of first-century culture, do risen visions or resurrectional apparitions, even if factual and historical, explain the birth of Christianity?

One final point. Visions and apparitions were not only an accepted commonplace possibility in the early first century, they are also an accepted commonplace possibility in the late twentieth century. In a paper presented to the 1995 spring meeting of the Jesus Seminar, Stacy Davids summarized recent psychiatric literature on grief and bereavement.

Review of well-conducted studies of the past three decades show that about one-half to eighty percent of bereaved people studied feel this intuitive, sometimes overwhelming "presence" or "spirit" of the lost person.... These perceptions happen most often in the first few months following the death but sometimes persist more than a year, with significantly more women than men reporting these events.... The American Psychiatric Association, author of *The Diagnostic and Statistical Manual of Mental Disorders-IV*, considers these phenomena (when "one hears the voice of, or transiently sees the image of, the deceased person") as nonpathological. They are viewed as common characteristics of uncomplicated grief, and not attributable to a mental disorder.... Part of the work of grief entails repeated, monotonous recalling of the events leading up to the death, as the mourner undergoes a restless need to "make sense; of what happened, to make it explicable, and to classify it along with other similar events.... During this process, accurate recording and telling of the dead person's life is of utmost importance to the bereaved.[34]

---

33. Celsus, *On the True Doctrine: A Discourse against the Christians*, ed. and trans. R. Joseph Hoffmann (New York: Oxford University Press, 1987), 57–58, 59, 68.

34. Stacy Davids, "Appearances of the Resurrected Jesus and the Experience of Grief," paper presented to the spring meeting of the Jesus Seminar, Santa Rosa, Calif., 1995, 3–6.

As I write these lines, Sebastian Junger's powerful elegy for those who go down at sea is deservedly high on the *New York Times* bestseller list for nonfiction. It centers on the *Andrea Gail*, a 72-foot steel swordfisher out of Gloucester which disappeared with all hands off Sable Island east of Nova Scotia, October 28, 1991, in waves 100 feet high. "If the men on the *Andrea Gail* had simply died, and their bodies were lying in state somewhere, their loved ones could make their goodbyes and get on with their lives. But they didn't die, they disappeared off the face of the earth and, strictly speaking, it's just a matter of faith that these men will never return." That comment and the epigraph above tell us what can happen today in contemporary America after any death but especially after a sudden, tragic, or mysterious one as intimates mourn their beloved dead. There are dreams and there are visions. Dale Murphy, who disappeared on the *Andrea Gail*, left a three-year-old son, Dale, an ex-wife, Debra, and a mother behind him. His son "wakes up screaming in the middle of the night" because "Daddy's in the room.... Daddy was just here.... Daddy was here and told me what happened on the boat." But adults, "too, are visited. [Dale Murphy's] mother looks out the bedroom window one day and sees Murph ambling down their street in huge deck boots. Someone else spots him in traffic in downtown Bradenton. From time to time Debra dreams that she sees him and runs up and says, 'Dale, where've you been?' And he won't answer, and she'll wake up in a cold sweat, remembering."[35]

Remember the statement about Christianity's birth that I suggested above: it is the resurrectional apparition of a dead man that explains the power of Christianity's birth and growth, spread and triumph, across the Roman empire. Here, however, is the problem. Why, against that early first-century context, does vision, apparition, or resurrection explain anything since such events were not considered absolutely extraordinary, let alone completely unique? Why, in this late twentieth-century context, do they explain anything if things are still the same? There *was* an easier time when anti-Christian secularists could claim that visions and apparitions of the dead were simple lies at worst and delusions at best. There was an easier time when pro-Christian fundamentalists could respond that in all of human history there was only this one unique case in which a human being had risen from the dead. Both sides admitted the abnormality of such events: one side said they could never happen, the other side said they had happened only once. They were twin sides of the same rationalist coin. Whether, therefore, we look from first or twentieth century, it is necessary to take another look at resurrection and apparition, at historical Jesus and risen Lord, and at Paul in 1 Corinthians 15.

---

35. Sebastian Junger, *The Perfect Storm* (New York: Norton, 1997), 213, 214.

DUALISM AND INCONSISTENCY

In 1 Corinthians 15 Paul discusses a very precise question: what sort of body did the risen Jesus have? But Paul could not answer such a question without revealing what he thought a "body" was or what types of "bodies" there were. Before focusing on Paul's answer in 1 Corinthians 15, therefore, I discuss here another Pauline text that touches on those preliminary presuppositions, and I read Paul in debate with his recent provocative interpretation by Daniel Boyarin. In what follows, then, I keep Paul's Gal. 3:28, "There is no longer Jew or Greek, there is no longer slave or free, there is no longer male and female; for all of you are one in Christ Jesus," in tensile dialectic with Boyarin's *Carnal Israel*:

> Some Christians (whether Jewish or Gentile) could declare that there is no Greek or Jew, no male or female. No rabbinic Jew could do so, because people are bodies, not spirits, and precisely bodies are marked as male or female, and also marked, though bodily practices and techniques such as circumcision and food taboos, as Jew or Greek as well.[36]

Furthermore, I emphasize an inconsistency in Paul's acceptance of Hellenistic dualism which is most obvious in Gal. 3:28 and thence can be seen more clearly in 1 Corinthians 15. I begin, then, with a letter Paul wrote from Ephesus in the early 50s C.E. to the Christian communities he had founded in Galatia.

Paul as a Radical Jew

When an ancient society is confronted with imperial modernization it can choose rejection or assimilation. But it can never take either option absolutely. It is always a case of where, when, what, and why to renounce or accept that alien intransigence. It is always a case of what is superficial and what is basic, of what is negotiable and what is intolerable. It is always a case of by whom and how that difference is decided. By the first common-era century, ancient traditional Judaism was under increasing pressures not just from Roman commercial exploitation in the age of Augustus but from Greek cultural domination since the age of Alexander the Great. Modernization for many *then* was Hellenization, Greek internationalism, just as modernization for many today is Americanization. Is that a matter of jets, computers, communications? Is it

---

36. Daniel Boyarin, *Carnal Israel: Reading Sex in Talmudic Culture* (Berkeley: University of California Press, 1993), 10.

a matter of sex, drugs, violence? Is it a matter of freedom, democracy, justice? Is it a matter of materialism, individualism, secularism, capitalism? How exactly can a venerable traditional society negotiate acceptance and rejection when faced with cultural, social, economic, and military domination? But especially, how can it withstand overwhelming *cultural* imperialism: Paul speaks, after all, of "Jew and Greek," not of "Jew and Roman." Boyarin's thesis has four major points.

First, in a 1994 book Daniel Boyarin termed Paul "a radical Jew" and summarized his purpose like this:

[1] Paul was motivated by a Hellenistic desire for the One, which among other things produced an ideal of a universal human essence, beyond difference and hierarchy. [2] This universal humanity, however, was predicated (and still is) on the dualism of the flesh and the spirit, such that while the body is particular, marked through practice as Jew or Greek, and through anatomy as male or female, the spirit is universal. [3] Paul did not, however, reject the body—as did, for instance, the gnostics—but rather promoted a system whereby the body had its place, albeit subordinated to the spirit.[37]

Later, the first two points of that thesis are repeated verbatim but there is a different final point: "[4] The strongest expression of this Pauline cultural criticism is Galatians and especially 3:28–29."[38] Those are, in other words, the four major and sequential points of his powerful thesis. Watch now as Judaism and Hellenism clash deep in Paul's sensibility and, without condescension at this safe distance, judge which is winning on the issue in question.

Second, that dualism of flesh and spirit derived from a pervasive Platonism in Paul's contemporary culture.

Various branches of Judaism (along with most of the surrounding culture) became increasingly platonized in late antiquity. By platonization I mean here the adoption of a dualist philosophy in which the phenomenal world was understood to be the representation in matter of a spiritual or ideal entity which corresponded to it. This has the further consequence that a hierarchical opposition is set up in which the invisible, inner reality is taken as more valuable or higher than the visible outer

<hr>

37. Daniel Boyarin, *A Radical Jew: Paul and the Politics of Identity* (Berkeley: University of California Press, 1994), 7, my numbering.
38. Ibid., 181, my numbering.

form of reality. In the anthropology of such a culture, the human person is constituted by an outer physical shell which is non-essential and by an inner spiritual soul, which represents his [*sic*] true and higher essence.[39]

That hierarchical dualism of spirit over flesh formed a spectrum from bodily neglect through bodily denigration to bodily rejection. The flesh could be to the spirit as its distracting mansion, its nomadic tent, its decrepit abode, or its filthy prison cell. Those were all points, however, along the same dualistic scale. Paul was not, for Boyarin, as radically dualistic as were the gnostics, but he had "as thoroughgoing a dualism as that of Philo," the contemporary Jewish philosopher from Alexandria, that is, "the body, while necessarily and positively valued by Paul is, as in Philo, not the human being but only his or her house or garment." Boyarin insists that Paul's dualism "does not imply a rejection of the body," it "does not abhor the body," it "makes room for the body, however much the spirit is more highly valued."[40] Paul stands, however, on a very slippery Hellenistic slope.

Third, Boyarin understands correctly that none of this has to do with "a Hellenistic Judaism which is somehow less pure than a putative 'Palestinian' Judaism."[41] It is not as if all of Palestinian Judaism was monistic and all of Hellenistic Judaism was dualistic. It is a difference not in geography but in ideology. It depended, wherever one lived, on the acceptance or rejection of that Platonic dualism and in what form or to what degree. Boyarin parallels Paul with Philo, but in case one might think that dualistic ideology is only for Diaspora Jews, I insert an example from Josephus, a Palestinian contemporary.

It is a rather striking example of Platonic dualism, of the spirit's transcendence over the body, and of the flesh's irrelevance to the soul. It is a speech placed by Josephus on the lips of Eleazar, leader of the besieged rebels atop Masada at the end of the First Roman War in 74 C.E. The Romans under Flavius Silva had built up a huge ramp against the isolated mesa-like rock fortress and the end was now in sight. The defenders decide to kill their families and then themselves. Eleazar encourages them to prefer death to slavery in *Jewish War* 7.344, 346.

> For it is death which gives liberty to the soul and permits it to depart to its own pure abode, there to be free from all calamity; but so long as it is imprisoned in a mortal body and tainted with all its miseries, it is, in

---

39. Ibid., 59. The "[*sic*]" is original.
40. Ibid., 59, 64, 185.
41. Ibid., 6.

sober truth, dead, for association with what is mortal ill befits that which is divine.... But it is not until, freed from the weight that drags it down to earth and clings about it, the soul is restored to its proper sphere, that it enjoys a blessed energy and a power untrammelled on every side, remaining, like God Himself, invisible to human eyes.

That speech, of course, is not Eleazar speaking to his fellow rebels but Josephus speaking to his fellow Romans. But it is hard to find a more precise formulation of the superiority of soul over body and of spirit over flesh. The question for first-century Jews was not whether one lived in Palestine or the Diaspora or whether one spoke Greek or Aramaic, but whether that person had absorbed ideologically that Hellenistic dualism as had Philo, Paul, and Josephus.

Fourth, since that "common dualist ideology... has characterized western thought practically since its inception" there "is... nothing striking in claiming that Paul was such a dualist; if anything the bold step that I am making is to claim that the Rabbis (as opposed to both earlier Hellenistic Jews and later ones) *resisted* this form of dualism." Boyarin uses the term *Rabbis* or *Rabbinic Judaism* "only with regard to the second century and onward" and their resistance to Platonic dualism is what he means by a "rejectionist" rather than an "assimilationist" reaction to Hellenization. "Of course," he says, "the Rabbis also believed in a soul that animates the body. The point is, rather, that they identified the human being not as a soul dwelling in a body but as a body animated by a soul, and that makes all the difference in the world."[42]

THE PROBLEM OF TERMINOLOGY

Monistic and Dualistic Traditions

That dichotomy between a monism of necessarily enfleshed spirit and a dualism of accidentally enfleshed spirit needs some precise descriptive terminology. Boyarin's analysis, which I find very persuasive, emphasizes a distinction between Platonized or Hellenized Judaism and traditional or rabbinical Judaism. In an earlier article I emphasized a distinction, within Christianity rather than Judaism, between gnostic and Catholic Christianity.[43] I am, however, no longer satisfied with that formulation of the difference between flesh-spirit

---

42. Boyarin, *Radical Jew*, 85, 2, 7, 278 n. 8.

43. John Dominic Crossan, "Why Christians Must Search for the Historical Jesus," *Bible Review* 12, no. 2 (April 1996): 34–38, 42–45.

monism and flesh/spirit dualism. On the one hand, it is better than Kurt Rudolph's distinction of Gnosis and Church: "One can almost say that Gnosis followed the Church like a shadow; the Church could never overcome it, its influence had gone too deep. By reason of their common history they remain two—hostile—sisters."[44] The trouble with that formulation is, on the one hand, that gnosis seems safely outside church rather than being, as in the bifurcation of gnostic Christianity and Catholic Christianity, options within the same church. The trouble with gnostic and Catholic Christianity, on the other, is that it is hardly coincident with the monism and dualism under discussion. Even if all of gnostic Christianity were dualistic, not all of Catholic Christianity was monistic. But the far deeper problem is Michael Williams's recent demand that we dismantle the dubious category of "gnosticism" itself.

Undemiurgical and Demiurgical Traditions

Williams proposes not just an alternative *term* for the too vague and too polemical "gnosticism" but an alternative *category,* which he defines at the start and end of his very powerful book:

> I would suggest the category "biblical demiurgical traditions" as one useful alternative. By "demiurgical" traditions I mean all those that ascribe the creation and management of the cosmos to some lower entity or entities, distinct from the highest God. This would include most of ancient Platonism, of course. But if we add the adjective "biblical," to denote "demiurgical" traditions that also incorporate or adapt traditions from Jewish or Christian Scripture, the category is narrowed significantly. In fact, the category "biblical demiurgical" would include a large percentage of the sources that today are usually called "gnostic," since the distinction between the creator(s) of the cosmos and the true God is normally identified as a common feature of "gnosticism."...
>
> I have suggested in this study at least one alternative. The category "biblical demiurgical" could be fairly clearly defined. It would include all sources that made a distinction between the creator(s) and controllers of the material world and the most transcendent divine being, and that in so doing made use of Jewish or Christian scriptural traditions. This category would not simply be a new name for "gnosticism," however,

---

44. Kurt Rudoph, *Gnosis*, trans. R. McL. Wilson, P. W. Coxon, and K. H. Kuhn, ed. Wilson (San Francisco: Harper and Row, 1983), 368.

since it would not precisely correspond to the grouping included in most anthologies of "gnostic" sources or discussions of this subject. There would indeed be considerable overlap, since the largest number of sources normally called "gnostic" also happen to contain or assume some biblical demiurgical myth.[45]

The category of "biblical demiurgical" is very helpful and may even explain something about origins as Bible met Demiurge and a spectrum of responses resulted:

> What I have called a demiurgical myth involves, after all, some presuppositions that were shared fairly widely in antiquity. That the world was administered and originally organized by a "middle management" level of the divine came to be taken for granted in most Platonic philosophy, for example, and at least by the beginning of the Common Era such a notion would have struck many people in the Greco-Roman world as perfectly sensible. In such an environment, it is not difficult to imagine why various Jews and/or Christians might have come to interpret biblical creation traditions accordingly.[46]

I accept Williams's category "biblical demiurgical" as more precise and accurate than the vastly overworked category "gnostic," but I still have one major question for that proposal. It is clear that the Creator God need not be either an evil rebel or an ignorant fool in a demiurgical tradition. But why is it always a lesser being than the High God? Why is it never an equal or even superior being? Put another way, if the biblical tradition in Judaism had a single High God who was also Creator God and the demiurgical tradition in Platonism had a Creator God separate and subordinate to the High God, what was involved in those divergent traditions? Williams says this:

> The definition of the category "biblical demiurgical" says nothing in itself about "anticosmism," and assumes nothing, and therefore it allows for the range of attitudes about the cosmos and its creator(s) that are actually attested in the works.[47]

---

45. Michael Allen Williams, *Rethinking "Gnosticism": An Argument for Dismantling a Dubious Category* (Princeton: Princeton University Press, 1996), 51–52, 265.

46. Ibid., 232.

47. Ibid., 265.

But does not demiurgical tradition and, therefore, biblical demiurgical tradition presume at least a separation and hierarchy of spirit over matter and soul over flesh? Why else is the Demiurge needed except to distance the High God from this low world? Not "anticosmism," maybe, but hardly procosmism either. Williams never discusses the divergent ideology or sensibility behind a demiurgical or nondemiurgical tradition.

Sarcophilic and Sarcophobic Traditions

In order to emphasize those divergent sensibilities I propose two categories, which are deliberately provocative and which intend to emphasize the historical effects of that disjunction which flowed from Platonism into (some) Judaism and (some) Christianity, and which is still present in our contemporary Western world wherever and whenever flesh is separated from spirit. Flesh can then be sensationalized and spirit can be sentimentalized. The result is that both are equally dehumanized. I call that monism of enfleshed spirit *sarcophilia*, and that dualism of flesh against spirit *sarcophobia*, from the Greek roots for "flesh" (*sarx*), "love" (*philia*), and "fear" (*phobos*). The terms are created on the analogy of sarcophagus, the marble coffin of antiquity, from "flesh" (*sarx*) and "eat" (*phagein*). We are dealing, I think, with a profound fault line in Western sensibility and consciousness. My own position is monistic rather than dualistic. Cosmic dualism separates spirit and matter, exalts spirit over matter, equates male with spirit and female with matter, and, in my view, dehumanizes our sexuality and our humanity in that process. We are spiritual flesh or fleshly spirit and we flee that amalgam at our peril. I admit this openly because both author *and reader* have to answer for their own sensibility before continuing this discussion.

Incarnational and Docetic Traditions

There is, however, a second and specifically Christian distinction that interacts with that one, but which could also have existed without it. It is also a difficult one for us to understand, but it connects with what was seen earlier about gods and goddesses assuming human bodies for business purposes here on earth. Some moderns may live in a world where immortal and mortal, heavenly and earthly, divine and human are rather transcendentally separated from one another. Not so, in general, for the ancients. Their world was filled with gods, goddesses, and spirits who assumed divergent shapes and figures, who assumed and changed bodies as we assume clothes and change styles. Gods and goddesses, for example, could appear in any material, animal, or human form appropriate for the occasion. But all such bodies were not *really* real. They were only *apparently* real. They are like the special-effects bodies on our movie screens. Could and did gods and goddesses become incarnate? Of course. They did so regularly, differently, and realistically, so that mortals could not recognize the unreality of those apparitional, illusional bodies. But did they really become incarnate? Of course not! That accepted unreality of divine flesh presented earliest Christianity with a serious and profound problem concerning Jesus. We might think to ourselves: of course Jesus was human. The question is: was he divine? They had the opposite problem. If they believed Jesus was divine, the question became: how could he be human? How could his body be real rather than apparitional and illusional? Was it not just a seem-to-be body?

There was no point in responding that people saw, heard, or even touched his body. For all those things could be, as it were, arranged by resident divinity. One obvious answer has been brilliantly explored by Gregory Riley.[48] Jesus could be explained not as *god* or *spirit* but as *hero*, as the offspring of a divine and human conjunction, himself therefore half-human and half-divine but really and truly each half. He could, as such, ascend after a real and true death to take his place among the heavenly immortals. But if one ever wished to move beyond Jesus as hero to Jesus as spirit or Jesus as god, the unreality of his flesh and the apparitional illusion of his body would have seemed inevitable concomitants in the ancient world.

If Jesus was divine, was his body real and *incarnational* in the sense of fully and validly enfleshed, or was his body unreal and apparitional, only seemingly enfleshed, a *docetic* body (from Greek *dokein*, "to seem")? The problem was not, as it might be for some of us, whether divine beings could walk this earth in human form, holding conversations, having intercourse, and producing children. Of course they could and did, but their bodies were but unreal play-bodies. When Christians composed, for example, that ancient and pre-Pauline hymn to Jesus in Phil. 2:6–11, were they imagining his body as real or apparitional, true or seeming so, normal or docetic? That distinction of, let us call it *incarnational*, as against *docetic* Christianity, would have existed even if the earlier and more basic one of *sarcophilic* as against *sarcophobic* Christianity had never occurred but, once both of them were present, they could interact unhappily ever after. That is what I meant at the start of this

48. Gregory John Riley, *One Jesus, Many Christs: How Jesus Inspired Not One True Christianity, but Many: The Truth about Christian Origins* (San Francisco: HarperSanFrancisco, 1997).

chapter by speaking of sarcophilic and/or incarnational as distinct from sarco-phobic and/or docetic Christianity. And with that terminology in place, I return to Boyarin and Paul in Gal. 3:28 before moving on, once again, to 1 Corinthians 15.

Ethnicity, Class, and Gender

How does that Platonic dualism apply, for Boyarin, to Paul's three distinctions of ethnicity, class, and gender, negated for Christians in Gal. 3:28? Against such a dualistic background those three negated distinctions could apply to the person-as-soul rather than to the nonperson-as-flesh. They could apply to rit-ual present or heavenly future but not to contemporary society or social real-ity. It is easy to imagine a Platonizing or Hellenizing Paul asserting that such physical or material disjunctions had nothing whatsoever to do with the soul, the spirit, the true human being. They were as irrelevant before God or in Christ as the color of one's hair or the shape of one's toes. That is the way Boyarin explains Paul. "What drove Paul was a passionate desire for human unification, for the erasure of differences and hierarchies between human beings, and... he saw the Christian event, as he had experienced it, as the vehi-cle for this transformation of humanity."[49] But if that was all Paul had done, if he had been consistently Hellenistic, we would still be yawning. His Jewish and Hellenistic genes fought not to a compromise but to an inconsistency. A compromise might have said that the flesh is to be kept in its inferior place but it is never to be totally rejected. An inconsistency is something else and that is what happens to Paul.

This is it. *He takes that first distinction of Jew and Gentile out of the soul and onto the body, out of the spirit and onto the flesh.* He takes ethnicity negation out into the streets of the Roman cities but he does not take class negation or gen-der negation outside in the same way. He does not say for ethnicity, as he does for class and gender, that it is irrelevant before God religiously and spiritually but should be maintained physically and socially. *The contradiction is not that he took all three spiritually but that he took one physically as well as spiritually.* If the Jew/Greek distinction was taken spiritually, it would mean that inside both were equal and that outside neither was significant. It would make no differ-ence, then, to be circumcised Jew or uncircumcised Greek. It would make no difference, *one way or the other.* To be not circumcised would be no better or worse than to be circumcised. But, to put it bluntly and practically, if Paul had

---

49. Boyarin, *Carnal Israel*, 106.

a son, he would not have circumcised him. Even though Gal. 5:6 and 6:15 insist that "neither circumcision nor uncircumcision" is important, not to circumcise *was* important for Paul. Circumcision is caustically termed "mutilation" in 5:12. Paul had earlier broken with James, Peter, Barnabas, and everyone else over minimal kosher observance so that Jewish Christians and Pagan Christians could eat together at Antioch in Gal. 2:11–14. Boyarin is quite right that Paul compromised between his Judaism and his Hellenism by adopting not a radical (rejection of flesh for spirit) but a moderate Platonic dualism (subordination of flesh to spirit). It is not that *compromise* I emphasize but the *inconsistency* with which he applies it to Gal. 3:28.

What is needed, from Paul then or Boyarin now, is to meditate on the *difference between those three differences*. And in that meditation the presence of the class distinction is crucial. For example, difference without hierarchy could be preserved in the case of ethnicity and gender, but not in the case of class. For class, difference is hierarchy and hierarchy is difference. The rich are different from the poor; they have more money. The free are different from the slaves; they have more power! Had Paul negated all three distinctions physically and materially in the urban streets of Roman cities, his life would have been as short as that of Jesus. Boyarin does not see that inconsistency in Paul. It is an inconsistency that allows Paul to negate Jew/Greek to the fullest physical extent concerning circumcision or kosher but to negate slave/free and male/female in a far more spiritual manner. The inconsistency on those three distinctions in Paul is matched by a similar one in Boyarin himself.

In the above quotation from his 1993 book, *Carnal Israel*, Boyarin mentions only the first and last of Paul's three distinctions, ethnicity, class, and gender, from Gal. 3:28. That could just have been a passing emphasis and omission were it not for what happens in his 1994 sequel, *A Radical Jew*, which is a total interpretation of Paul based on Gal. 3:28, "my key for unlocking Paul." But repeatedly, consistently, and without excuse or explanation, he omits the middle term *class* to concentrate exclusively on ethnicity and gender. The distinction of class is singled out for emphasis once, "there is no slave or free in Christ," with specific regard to Paul's letter to Philemon about his runaway slave, Onesimus. All three distinctions are mentioned a few times, for example, "in baptism, all the differences that mark off one body from another as Jew or Greek... male or female, slave or free, are effaced," or again, "behind Paul's ministry was a profound vision of a humanity undivided by ethnos, class, and sex," and again, "In Galatians Paul seems indeed to be wiping out social differences and hierarchies between the genders in addition to those that obtain between ethnic groups and socioeconomic classes."[50] But that is about all there is on the class distinction in a book that discusses brilliantly those of ethnicity and gender. I emphasize that point, for both Paul and Boyarin, because if we consider the difference between those three differences, and the difference between difference and hierarchy, we will have to face these questions. If differences of ethnicity and gender can exist without hierarchy, can it be the same for class? How is class different from ethnicity and gender? Paul never asked those questions, and neither does Boyarin. And because of that failure, Boyarin recognizes clearly Paul's dualism but fails completely to recognize the inconsistency with which Paul applies that dualism. It is not just that dualism but especially that inconsistency that I focus on as I return, finally, to 1 Corinthians 15. I do not use terms like *dualism* or *inconsistency* with any sense of superiority or condescension because, for Paul, they are powerful and generative forces created by swimming hard in the riptides of history. We should not, however, simply repeat them but develop further their profoundly human challenge.

THE BODILY RESURRECTION OF JESUS

Paul is still at Ephesus in the early 50s C.E., but now he is writing westward to Corinth rather than eastward to Galatia. His Corinthian converts are proper Platonic dualists who have no problem with Jesus as resurrected soul or immortal spirit. But how can he possibly have a body and why would he want one in any case? Why tell a prisoner he will get back his cell for all eternity? Who needs an immortal burden? Soul yes, body no. Spirit yes, flesh no.

In 1 Corinthians 15 Paul begins by enumerating all the apparitions of the risen Jesus. But, having recited them in 15:1–11, he never mentions them again throughout the rest of the argument in 15:12–58. The reason is quite clear. The Corinthians know all about visions and apparitions and would not dream about denying their validity. Of course the shades return from below with visible and even tangible bodies. Of course the immortals, born of human and divine parents and assumed among the gods and goddesses after death, return from above with visible and even tangible bodies. Of course the gods and goddesses assume bodies to contact mortals, to make love, to make war, to make conversation. But those are seeming-bodies, play-bodies, in-appear-ance-only bodies. They are not made from flesh and blood but from ether and air. Notice, by the way, that we use *body* and *flesh* more or less interchangeably but that a dualistic sensibility could easily concede that divinities, immortals, or spirits had bodies but not flesh. It is, as suggested earlier, somewhat like our

---

50. Boyarin, *Radical Jew*, 23, 5, 181, 183.

special-effects movies today. There are times we are seeing body but not flesh, as it were. Those dinosaurs do not digest. In what follows, Paul is trying to hold on to something clearly important for him but watch, once again, how compromise begets inconsistency.

The question could not be clearer in 15:35: "But someone will ask, 'How are the dead raised? With what kind of body do they come?'" Paul interweaves two answers, one fairly conventional, the other more challenging. The conventional one claims that there are a lot of different body types. The stars, for example, moved and so they were living beings with bodies. But their bodies were immortal unlike our own. There is even, Paul claims, such a thing as "a spiritual body." Most Hellenistic hearers would consider the bodies of apparitional divinities as "spiritual" rather than "physical." They hung them up like clothes, as it were, at the end of the operation. New ones, different ones, vegetable, animal, or mineral ones, were created as needed. But there is also for another answer, the metaphor of sowing, in 1 Cor. 15:36–44:

> Fool! What you sow does not come to life unless it dies. And as for what you sow, you do not sow the body that is to be, but a bare seed, perhaps of wheat or of some other grain. But God gives it a body as he has chosen, and to each kind of seed its own body. Not all flesh is alike, but there is one flesh for human beings, another for animals, another for birds, and another for fish. There are both heavenly bodies and earthly bodies, but the glory of the heavenly is one thing, and that of the earthly is another. There is one glory of the sun, and another glory of the moon, and another glory of the stars; indeed, star differs from star in glory. So it is with the resurrection of the dead. What is sown is perishable, what is raised is imperishable. It is sown in dishonor, it is raised in glory. It is sown in weakness, it is raised in power. It is sown a physical body, it is raised a spiritual body. If there is a physical body, there is also a spiritual body.

The metaphor of multiple body types emphasizes only difference but the metaphor of sowing emphasizes both continuity and divergence. What is sown is both absolutely the same and completely different from what is reaped. It is not possible to sow a fish and reap a bird. Sow a specific seed and reap a specific ear of grain. That is the present inconsistency that I see arising from Paul's Platonic compromise. There is, of course, spiritual continuity between the earthly Jesus and the heavenly Christ. No one at Corinth debates that. But is there bodily continuity—that is, physical and material—continuity between them? Paul wavers in response. If focus is on those different body types, the answer is no: Jesus once had a physical body, Jesus now has a spiritual body. If focus is on the seed metaphor, the answer is yes: Jesus is now both totally the same and absolutely different. The Corinthians probably focused on that "spiritual body" and understood it as meaning a body, air-woven as it were, like divinities, immortals, and shades assumed for human contacts. They would be reassured of that interpretation when Paul concluded with this comment, in 1 Cor. 15:50: "What I am saying, brothers and sisters, is this: flesh and blood cannot inherit the kingdom of God, nor does the perishable inherit the imperishable."

There might be different types of bodies but there was only one type of flesh-and-blood body. It was flesh and blood that bothered the Platonic dualist; spiritual bodies were quite acceptable. In all of that, I can hold on only to Paul's seed metaphor because there, for a moment, the compromise is negated and his Judaism speaks aloud. The seed that is sown and the grain that is produced are both same and different and are in unbroken material and physical continuity. But that is only a passing Jewish-Jewish inconsistency in a generally Hellenistic-Jewish explanation. Nevertheless, since I myself find Platonic dualism, in any degree and by whatever name, to be fundamentally dehumanizing, I hold on to that inconsistency and ask what else, besides such dualism, is at work in Paul.

The earthly Jesus was not just a thinker with ideas but a rebel with a cause. He was a Jewish peasant with an attitude and he claimed his attitude was that of the Jewish God. But it was, he said, in his life and in ones like it that the Kingdom of God was revealed, that the Jewish god of justice and righteousness was incarnated in a world of injustice and unrighteousness. The Kingdom was never just about words and ideas, aphorisms and parables, sayings and dialogues. It was about a way of life. And that means it was about a flesh-and-blood body. Justice is always about bodies and lives, not just about words and ideas. Resurrection does not mean, simply, that the spirit or soul of Jesus lives on in the world. And neither does it mean, simply, that the companions or followers of Jesus live on in the world. *It must be the embodied life that remains as powerfully efficacious in this world.* I recognize those claims as a historian and I believe them as a Christian. There is, then, only one Jesus, the embodied Galilean who lived a life of divine justice in an unjust world, who was officially and legally executed by that world's accredited representatives, and whose continued empowering presence indicates, for believers, that God is not on the side of injustice, even, or especially, imperial injustice. There are not two Jesuses, one pre-Easter and another post-Easter, one earthly and another heavenly, one with a physical and another with a spiritual body. There is only one Jesus, the *historical* Jesus who incarnated, for believers, the Jewish God of justice in a community of such life back then and continued to do so ever afterwards.

With that understanding, I accept Paul's seed metaphor as very helpful. From seed to grain is a combination of something absolutely the same and yet totally different. So with resurrection. It is the same Jesus, the one and only historical Jesus of the late 20s in his Jewish homeland, but now untrammeled by time and place, language and proximity. It is the one and only Jesus, absolutely the same, absolutely different. He is trammeled, of course, then, now, and always, by faith. Bodily resurrection has nothing to do with a resuscitated body coming out of its tomb. And neither is it just another word for Christian faith itself. Bodily resurrection means that the embodied life and death of the historical Jesus continues to be experienced, by believers, as powerfully efficacious and salvifically present in this world. That life continues, as it always has, to form communities of like lives.

In the light of all that, the title of this section should be not the *bodily* resurrection of Jesus but the *fleshly* resurrection of Jesus. I tend to use those words interchangeably but Paul most certainly does not and it is now clear why he would not. When, therefore, he says that "flesh and blood" cannot enter the Kingdom of God, a gulf in sensibility opens up between him and Jesus (and between him and me, to be honest). For Jesus, anyone incarnating divine justice on earth was "flesh and blood" entering the Kingdom of God. And such a person should expect that flesh to be separated from that blood as punishment for that entrance. Paul is also in contradiction to the declaration in John 1:14 that "the Word became flesh and lived among us." The Word, *Logos* in Greek, means the intelligibility of the world, the rationality of the universe, the meaning of life, as revelation of the Divine Mind. And John says it became not just body but flesh, not just the special-effects *body* of standard Greco-Roman divine visitations, but the one and only flesh and blood of full and normal human existence. The *Word* became *flesh*, that is to say, the divine meaning of life is incarnated in a certain human way of living.

I conclude with the image of a body destroyed with cruel contempt, public ignominy, and intended annihilation. The Easter issues of *Newsweek*, *Time*, as well as *U.S. News and World Report* (April 8, 1996) all had cover stories on the historical Jesus. *Newsweek* had the caption, "Rethinking the Resurrection: A New Debate about the Risen Christ." It was written across a picture of Jesus rising heavenwards, arms uplifted, hands facing outwards. What struck me immediately as strange was the complete absence of any wounds on those clearly visible hands and feet. I failed to realize that they had mistakenly taken Jesus from a Transfiguration instead of a Resurrection painting. There were, of course, no wounds on that Vatican work by Raphael because it depicted an event before the death of Jesus. *U.S. News and World Report*, on the other hand (no pun intended), had a correct picture. Its cover had the caption "In Search of Jesus: Who Was He? New Appraisals of His Life and Meaning?" written across Jesus from a Bellini painting of the resurrection with the wound in Jesus' right hand clearly visible. Think, now, about those wounds.

There is, ever and always, only one Jesus. For sarcophilic and/or incarnational Christianity that is the historical Jesus *as* risen Jesus. And the test is this: does the risen Jesus still carry the wounds of crucifixion? In the gospel, art, and mysticism of sarcophilic and/or incarnational Christianity, the answer is clearly in the affirmative. But those wounds came not from heaven but from history. Imagine a stranger from afar looking at Bellini's painting and asking why that man had holes in his hands. He would need an explanation of the *death* of Jesus, but not just about any type of death. It was not death by, say, disease or drowning, illness or accident. It was by official Roman execution reserved for lower-class subversives. So, the questioner might respond, *he* must have been a particularly dangerous criminal? Or so, the questioner might respond, *they* must have been a particularly evil people. He would need an explanation about the *life* of Jesus, that is, about the historical Jesus within the context of Jewish resistance to imperial injustice.

With those canonical gospels as inaugural models and primordial examples, each Christian generation must write its gospels anew, must first reconstruct its historical Jesus with fullest integrity, and then say and live what that reconstruction means for present life in this world. History and faith are always a dialectic for incarnational Christianity. Put otherwise, its insistence on the resurrection of Jesus' flesh is my insistence on the permanence of Jesus' history. But then, now, and always it is history seen by faith.

2

The Humanity of Jesus

What's at Stake in the Quest for the Historical Jesus

Luke Timothy Johnson

The quest for the historical Jesus is itself a most peculiar historical phenomenon. Despite the impression that might be given by the news media and even some contemporary questers, this form of intellectual inquiry has been going on with varying degrees of intensity since the early eighteenth century.[1] Albert Schweitzer's classic 1906 account of the quest from Reimarus to Wrede was itself a very large book, even though his survey was by no means complete.[2] Schweitzer's analysis of the quest also seemed for a time to end it.[3] But the quest began again as a small trickle in the 1960s,[4] eventually became a major tributary,[5] and is now again in full flood, with new versions of Jesus available at Barnes and Noble almost monthly.[6]

---

1. Charlotte Allen, *The Human Christ: The Quest for the Historical Jesus* (New York: Free Press, 1998), 92–119, shows the way such late-seventeenth- and early-eighteenth-century freethinkers as Anthony Collins, Matthew Tindale, John Toland, and above all, Thomas Chubb anticipated most later versions of the historical Jesus.

2. A. Schweitzer, *The Quest of the Historical Jesus: A Critical Study of Its Progress from Reimarus to Wrede*, trans. W. Montgomery, with a new introduction by J. M. Robinson (New York: Macmillan, 1968). Schweitzer concentrated primarily on the quest within German scholarship, with a side glance to such French productions as Renan's *Vie de Jesus* (1863). To augment Schweitzer's account, see M. Goguel, *Jesus and the Origins of Christianity*, vol. 1: *Prolegomena to the Life of Jesus*, trans. O. Wyon (1932; New York: Harper and Brothers, 1960), 37–69; Allen, *The Human Christ*; and D. Pals, *The Victorian "Lives" of Jesus* (San Antonio, Tex.: Trinity University Press, 1982). The peculiar manifestations of the American scene are well catalogued by P. Allitt, "The American Christ," *American Heritage* (November 1988): 128–41.

48

The question I want to pose is the simplest one imaginable. Why is there such a quest for the historical Jesus? The question is simple but has several parts. Why, after some seventeen centuries of Christianity, did it suddenly seem important to inquire historically into the figure of Jesus? Why did so

---

3. Schweitzer had shown on one hand that much of the earlier Jesus research was a form of projection in which investigators found in Jesus an idealized version of themselves. On the other hand, he concluded that genuine historical research must choose between two unhappy options: either the gospels are utterly unreliable regarding the identity and ministry of Jesus, or (if they are reliable) the Jesus they present is so totally different from the present as to be unassimilable. In suggesting, however, that what is of eternal validity in Jesus is his speech that can communicate to each individual at any time his own eschatological vision of reality, Schweitzer also pointed the way to a renewed search (see *Quest*, 401–2).

4. Within German scholarship, the influence of Bultmann and Barth helped delay a renewed quest, even though Bultmann's *Jesus and the Word*, trans. L. P. Smith and E. H. Lantero (New York: Scribner's, 1958), was a significant response to Schweitzer's implied invitation. Within the Bultmann school, E. Käsemann's 1953 lecture, "The Problem of the Historical Jesus" (see *Essays on New Testament Themes*, trans. W. J. Montague [Philadelphia: Fortress Press, 1964], 15–47), was pivotal. Käsemann sought a position between the skepticism of Bultmann and the positivism of such questers as E. Stauffer, *Jesus and His Story*, trans. Richard and Clara Winston (New York: Knopf, 1960), and Joachim Jeremias, *New Testament Theology: The Proclamation of Jesus*, trans. J. Bowden (New York: Scribner's, 1971); see E. Käsemann, "Blind Alleys in the 'Jesus of History' Controversy," *New Testament Questions of Today*, trans. W. J. Montague (Philadelphia: Fortress Press, 1969), 23–65. The prospects for a new quest were sketched for American scholars by J. M. Robinson, *A New Quest of the Historical Jesus*, Studies in Biblical Theology 23 (London: SCM Press, 1959), who also provided valuable bibliographical information on the search between the time of Schweitzer and Käsemann (see pp. 9–25).

5. More accurately, perhaps, a series of tributaries that intersected and interconnected in several ways and at several stages. Two can be noted in particular. The first has specialized in dissecting layers of narrative materials in order to find those sayings of Jesus that are regarded as authentic. Here we find the work of Jeremias and his successors on the parables (see, e.g., J. Jeremias, *The Parables of Jesus*, trans. from 6th ed. by S. H. Hooke [New York: Scribner's, 1963]; J. D. Crossan, *In Parables: The Challenge of the Historical Jesus* [New York: Harper and Row, 1973]; D. O. Via, *The Parables: Their Literary and Existential Dimension* [Philadelphia: Fortress Press, 1967]; and R. Funk, *Parable and Presence: Forms of the New Testament Tradition* [Philadelphia: Fortress Press, 1982]); of Perrin on other sayings of Jesus (see *Rediscovering the Teachings of Jesus* [New York: Harper and Row, 1967]), and eventually the work of Robert Funk and the Jesus Seminar (see R. W. Funk and R. Hoover, *The Five Gospels: The Search for the Authentic Words of Jesus* [New York: Macmillan, 1993]). The other has developed out of Schweitzer's eschatological emphasis and has

many presumably meticulous scholars using the same methods applied to the same materials come up with such dramatically different results? Why after so much attention, energy, and intelligence devoted to the quest does it not appear to have reached a conclusion much to anyone's satisfaction? And finally, in the light of the quest's obvious inherent difficulties and the failure of all

---

sought to interpret Jesus' mission within the context of a reconstructed Judaism. Here we find among others the work of E. P. Sanders, *Jesus and Judaism* (Philadelphia: Fortress Press, 1985); Sanders, *The Historical Figure of Jesus* (London: Allen Lane, 1993); G. Vermes, *Jesus the Jew: A Historian's Reading of the Gospels* (Philadelphia: Fortress Press, 1983); Vermes, *Jesus and the World of Judaism* (London: SCM Press, 1983); J. Riches, *The World of Jesus: First Century Judaism in Crisis* (Cambridge: Cambridge University Press, 1990); R. A. Horsley, *Jesus and the Spiral of Violence: Popular Jewish Resistance in Roman Palestine* (San Francisco: Harper and Row, 1987); J. H. Charlesworth, *Jesus within Judaism: New Light from Exciting Archeological Discoveries* (Garden City, N.Y.: Doubleday, 1988); and N. T. Wright, *Jesus and the Victory of God*, Christian Origins and the Question of God 2 (Minneapolis: Fortress Press, 1996). For a helpful guide, see B. Witherington, *The Jesus Quest: The Third Search for the Jew of Nazareth* (Downer's Grove, Ill.: Intervarsity Press, 1995).

6. In L. T. Johnson, *The Real Jesus: The Misguided Quest for the Historical Jesus and the Truth of the Traditional Gospels* (San Francisco: HarperSanFrancisco, 1996), I survey the work of the Jesus Seminar and the productions of Barbara Thiering, *Jesus and the Riddle of the Dead Sea Scrolls: Unlocking the Secrets of His Life Story* (San Francisco: HarperSanFrancisco, 1992); John Spong, *Born of a Woman: A Bishop Rethinks the Birth of Jesus* (San Francisco: HarperSanFrancisco, 1992); Spong, *Resurrection: Myth or Reality?* (San Francisco: HarperSanFrancisco, 1994); A. N. Wilson, *Jesus* (New York: Norton, 1992); Stephen Mitchell, *The Gospel according to Jesus* (New York: HarperCollins, 1991); Marcus Borg, *Jesus, a New Vision: Spirit, Culture, and the Life of Discipleship* (San Francisco: Harper and Row, 1987); Borg, *Meeting Jesus Again for the First Time: The Historical Jesus and the Heart of Contemporary Faith* (San Francisco: HarperSanFrancisco, 1994); John Dominic Crossan, *The Historical Jesus: The Life of a Mediterranean Jewish Peasant* (San Francisco: HarperSanFrancisco, 1991); Crossan, *Jesus: A Revolutionary Biography* (San Francisco: HarperSanFrancisco, 1994); Crossan, *The Essential Jesus* (San Francisco: HarperSanFrancisco, 1994); Crossan, *Who Killed Jesus? Exposing the Roots of Anti-Semitism in the Gospel Story of the Death of Jesus* (San Francisco: HarperSanFrancisco, 1995); and John P. Meier, *A Marginal Jew: Rethinking the Historical Jesus*: vol. 1, *The Roots of the Problem and the Person* (New York: Doubleday, 1991), and vol. 2, *Mentor, Message, and Miracle* (New York: Doubleday, 1994). Because of the decision to restrict my focus, I was not able to touch on such other fascinating examples as J. Bowden, *Jesus: The Unanswered Questions* (Nashville: Abingdon Press, 1989); Morton Smith, *Jesus the Magician* (San Francisco: Harper and Row, 1978); and H. Boers, *Who Was Jesus? The Historical Jesus and the Synoptic Gospels* (San Francisco: Harper and Row, 1989). For a more positive view of many of these same books, see now R. Shorto, *Gospel Truth: The New Image of Jesus Emerging from Science and History, and Why It Matters* (New York: Putnam's Sons, 1997).

previous efforts, why does the quest not only continue today but flourish to an extent that, to some observers, makes it seem a topic uniquely capable of generating passion among biblical scholars?

Schweitzer's powerful analysis of the first quest provided some answers to these questions. The historical study of Jesus began due to the Enlightenment in Europe. At the time, two related convictions became popular among those considering themselves to live in an age of reason.[7] The first was that for religion to be true it had to be reasonable;[8] the second was that history was the most reasonable measure of truth.[9] The claims of Christians about Jesus must therefore also meet those standards. Not surprisingly, the quest for Jesus was driven most by those deeply dissatisfied with a Christianity that grounded its supernaturalism and sacramentalism in the figure of Jesus, and who therefore sought in a purely rational Jesus the basis for a Christianity purged of its superstitious elements.[10] The deist Thomas Jefferson perfectly represented this desire in his scissoring out of the gospels anything that smacked of the superstitious or supernatural in order to find in its pages a Jesus who was a simple teacher of morality applicable to all humans.[11]

That first search yielded such unsatisfactory results because there are major obstacles to determining what is historical about Jesus.[12] Although generous

---

7.   The task is provided impetus, of course, by the realization that the "biblical world" is not coextensive with "the real world," a realization that was forced on consciousness both by science and by world exploration. The presumption that the biblical world was simply descriptive of the real world could no longer naively be maintained; in some fashion, faith was now required to respond to the discourse of science and history in a more fundamental manner. On this, see H. Frei, *The Eclipse of Biblical Narrative: A Study in Eighteenth and Nineteenth Century Hermeneutics* (New Haven: Yale University Press, 1974).

8.   The first casualty was the miraculous element in biblical stories, challenged by the rationalists and decisively jettisoned by D. F. Strauss in his *Life of Jesus Critically Examined* (1835). What was not appreciated for a considerable length of time was the way that the definition of "miracle" in terms of the breaking of the "laws of nature" was already a fundamental capitulation to a Newtonian universe that is itself challengable on a number of grounds; see, e.g., W. Placher, *The Domestication of Transcendence: How Modern Thinking about God Went Wrong* (Louisville, Ky.: John Knox/Westminster Press, 1996), and S. Maitland, *A Big-Enough God: A Feminist's Search for a Joyful Theology* (New York: Henry Holt, 1995).

9.   See Schweitzer, *Quest*, 13–57; Allen, *The Human Christ*, 92–119. Once more, a legitimate premise—history has to do with human events in time and space and can therefore speak only about such events—can imperceptibly turn into an illegitimate inference: what history cannot speak about does not or cannot exist. To take only the most obvious example, if the resurrection cannot be demonstrated historically, the resurrection must not be real. There are actually two fallacies here. The first makes the historian's capacity to demonstrate an event of the past the test of its occurrence. The second makes history the sole legitimate way to apprehend reality.

compared to what we have for some ancient figures, the evidence concerning Jesus is still slender and fragmentary. From outside observers we have only enough to support the historicity of his place and time, mode of death, and movement.[13] The rest of our evidence comes from insiders, all of whom considered Jesus not to be a figure of the past alone, but above all a presence more powerfully alive and active because of his resurrection than before his death.[14]

Everything they wrote about him was colored by these convictions. There are seemingly intractable limits to the degree any search can disentangle what really happened from such biased sources.[15] The two basic options are to use

---

10. For examples, see P. Gay, *Deism: An Anthology* (Princeton: D. Van Nostrand, 1968), and in particular, Thomas Chubb, *The True Gospel of Jesus Christ Asserted* (London: Thomas Cox, 1737). See also W. Baird, *History of New Testament Research*, vol. 1, *From Deism to Tübingen* (Minneapolis: Fortress Press, 1992), 31–57. For the most explicit contemporary expression of the same position, see R. Funk, *Honest to Jesus: Jesus for a New Millennium* (San Francisco: HarperSanFrancisco, 1996), 23–29, 300–314.

11. Thomas Jefferson, *The Life and Morals of Jesus of Nazareth* (Washington, D.C.: USGPO, 1904; New York: Henry Holt, 1995).

12. See my *The Real Jesus*, 105–26.

13. The primary Jewish sources are Josephus, *Antiquities* 18.3.3, 18.5.2, and 20.9.1; and scattered references in the *Babylonian Talmud* (e.g., *Sanhedrin* 43a and 106a). The Greco-Roman sources are Suetonius' *Life of Claudius* 25.4, Tacitus' *Annals* 15.44.2–8, Pliny the Younger, *Letters* 10.96, and Lucian of Samosata, *Proteus Peregrinus* 11–13. By the late second century, the attack on Christians by Celsus' *True Word* reflects knowledge of earlier sources.

14. The point deserves underscoring: noncanonical writings are, if anything, even more "mythological" in their view of Jesus than are the canonical. By no means do they diminish the "resurrection/faith" perspective, even though they may understand it differently. In none of these extracanonical sources is Jesus regarded as merely human. Even the Jewish-Christian gospel fragments associated with the Ebionites or Nazoreans have explicit mention of the resurrection (see E. Hennecke, *New Testament Apocrypha*, vol. 1, *Gospels and Related Writings*, ed. W. Schneemelcher, trans. R. McL. Wilson [Philadelphia: Westminster Press, 1963], 117–65).

15. For a short discussion of the criteria used to sift authentic from inauthentic among the sayings of Jesus, see my *The Real Jesus*, 20–27, 128–33. In addition to the intrinsic difficulties attending any effort to trace the stages of any tradition in the absence of controls, it is too seldom noted that the entire selection of material now available to scholars derives from those who shared the resurrection perspective. The best such methods can do, furthermore, is determine the earliest form of a tradition, not whether a specific saying actually derived from Jesus. Finally, the results of such demonstration do not themselves constitute the set of all that Jesus might have said and done, but only a subset of a preselected body of sayings. Even if *their* authenticity is demonstrated, that does not by itself disqualify the authenticity of other sayings that the investigator cannot verify by such criteria.

the narrative framework of the gospels while trying to correct them for bias and implausibility, or to abandon the gospel framework and salvage some of the more historically plausible pieces from the wreckage. Since the gospel narratives themselves disagree both in content and sequence, the first option requires making choices between them.[16] Disregarding their narrative altogether, however, means that some other plausible framework must be found for the pieces of the Jesus tradition which one has deemed authentic.[17]

The first option was followed by most classical historians and early questers.[18] The procedure raises the question whether one has been sufficiently critical, or whether one has simply retold the biblical story.[19] The second option, favored by more recent questers, raises the question whether the selection of certain pieces and the fitting of them to new patterns is anything more than an imaginative exercise that reveals much more about the arranger than about Jesus.[20]

This brings us to the question why so many scholars using the same methods on the same materials have ended with such wildly divergent portraits of Jesus. To list only a few that have emerged: Jesus as romantic visionary (Renan), as eschatological prophet (Schweitzer, Wright), as wicked priest from

---

16. There is no need here to demonstrate what is immediately evident to anyone opening the pages of a synopsis: the gospels of Matthew, Mark, and Luke share a substantial amount of material, language, and order of presentation, but they also vary substantially in all three; John's gospel differs so markedly that it ordinarily does not appear in a synopsis.

17. A collection of sayings does not by itself constitute a coherent identity; for that, some sort of narrative framework is required. Once the narrative of the gospels has been dismissed as an invention of the evangelist, and once the construal of Jesus offered by the New Testament epistolary literature has been dismissed as irrelevant, then the way is open to using some other sociological or anthropological model as the framework within which the "authentic pieces" can be fitted.

18. Thus, the first quest eliminated John in favor of the Synoptics and then sought (through the solution of the "Synoptic Problem") to determine which of the three Synoptics was likely to have been the earliest—and presumably, best—source for the life of Jesus.

19. An egregious example is A. N. Wilson's *Jesus*, which basically moves through the four accounts, picking from them eclectically to construct what seems to the author to be a plausible sequence of events. The absence of any criterion for selection beyond personal taste does not appear to embarrass the writer.

20. The main examples here are J. D. Crossan, *The Historical Jesus*, who tries to get as much mileage as possible out of the designation of Jesus as "a Mediterranean Jewish Peasant," and M. Borg, who invokes the categories of "charismatic *chasid*" and "Revitalization Movement Founder" to provide controls for his selection of evidence.

Qumran (Thiering), as husband of Mary Magdalen (Spong), as revolutionary zealot (S. F. G. Brandon), as agrarian reformer (Yoder), as revitalization movement founder and charismatic (Borg), as gay magician (Smith), as cynic sage (Downing), as peasant thaumaturge (Crossan), as peasant poet (Bailey), and as guru of oceanic bliss (Mitchell).[21] The common element seems still to be the ideal self-image of the researcher. It is this tendency that led T. W. Manson to note sardonically, "By their lives of Jesus ye shall know them."[22]

In the light of such difficulties and such mixed results it is appropriate to ask why historical Jesus research, far from ceasing in fatigue or frustration, is flourishing. The answer cannot be simply that, like the Matterhorn or Everest for the mountain climber, Jesus is simply "there" as a subject who must be considered by any self-respecting historian. Historical Jesus research, in fact, is not primarily carried out by professional secular students of antiquity. For the most part, they show themselves remarkably ready to follow the storyline of the gospels as a reliable sketch of Jesus' ministry, and the account of Christian origins in the Acts of the Apostles as at least fundamentally credible.[23] The need to keep scratching at these sources seems to be an itch felt mainly by Christian scholars, who mix a considerable amount of theological interest into their history.[24]

---

21. S. G. F. Brandon, *Jesus and the Zealots* (New York: Scribner's, 1967); J. H. Yoder, *The Politics of Jesus: Vicit Agnus Noster* (Grand Rapids, Mich.: Eerdmans, 1973); G. F. Downing, *Christ and the Cynics: Jesus and Other Radical Preachers in First-Century Tradition* (Sheffield: Sheffield Academic Press, 1988); Crossan's *Jesus: A Revolutionary Life*, where the thaumaturgic element is stressed much more; K. E. Bailey, *Poet and Peasant, and Through Peasant Eyes: A Literary Cultural Approach to the Parables in Luke* (Grand Rapids, Mich.: Eerdmans, 1983).

22. T. W. Manson, "The Failure of Liberalism to Interpret the Bible as the Word of God," in *The Interpretation of the Bible,* ed. C. W. Dugmore (London: SPCK, 1944), 92. See also Martin Kähler: "What is usually happening is that the image of Jesus is being refracted through the spirit of these gentlemen themselves," in his *The So-Called Historical Jesus and the Historic, Biblical Christ,* trans. C. Braaten (1892; Philadelphia: Fortress Press, 1964), 56.

23. See, e.g., M. Grant, *Jesus: A Historian's Review of the Gospels* (New York: Scribner's, 1977), and A. N. Sherwin-White, *Roman Society and Roman Law in the New Testament* (Oxford: Clarendon Press, 1963).

24. Schweitzer noted of the first quest: "The historical investigation of the life of Jesus did not take its rise from a purely historical interest; it turned to the Jesus of history as an ally in the struggle against the tyranny of dogma" (*Quest,* 4). In this respect, the first quest was simply one aspect of the self-understanding of historical criticism as carried out by Christian (and above all, Protestant) scholars, namely to complete the Reformation by isolating by means of historical analysis that essential core of Christianity by which all forms of Christianity should be measured. Built into this perception are two premises that were seldom challenged: that the origins of a religion

Perhaps the renewal of historical Jesus research in the past two decades has derived from a sense that the advance of knowledge now makes success more likely than it had been in the previous quests.[25] This century, after all, has been one of unparalleled growth in discoveries about the ancient Mediterranean world. All this information, however, while wonderfully illuminating virtually every aspect of life in Jesus' world, does not add substantially to our knowledge of his life in that world.[26] The archaeological discoveries at Qumran and at Nag-Hammadi created those expectations at first, but most scholars today regard them of limited value for knowledge about Jesus.[27] It is also true that many of the contemporary questers place great stock on the Coptic *Gospel of Thomas* found at Nag-Hammadi as a new source of information for Jesus,[28] but they have convinced each other more than they have the rest of scholars that the *Gospel of Thomas* truly is a source for the sayings of Jesus as early as the canonical gospels rather than a composition dependent on them.[29]

---

define its essence, and that the nature of religion can be defined by historical criteria. On the presence of Protestant theological tendencies in the study of earliest Christianity, see J. Z. Smith, *Drudgery Divine: On the Comparison of Early Christianities and the Religions of Late Antiquity* (Chicago: University of Chicago Press, 1990), 1–35, and L. T. Johnson, *Religious Experience: A Missing Dimension in New Testament Studies* (Minneapolis: Fortress Press, 1998).

25. According to J. M. Robinson, *New Quest*, the availability of "new sources" is one of the reasons for a new quest (59–63).

26. From the side of the Greco-Roman world, this new knowledge is most impressively displayed by Crossan, *The Historical Jesus*, and from the side of Judaism, by Sanders, *Jesus and Judaism*.

27. The presence of an eschatologically defined community of Jewish sectarians within a few miles of the place of John's baptizing ministry remains tantalizing, just as the presence of the Hellenistic city of Sepphoris just a few miles from Jesus' home town of Nazareth remains intriguing. But it is no more provable that Jesus was connected to Qumran (though he may have been) than it is that he worked as a carpenter in Sepphoris and thereby learned Greek aphorisms (though he may have). Historians, fortunately or unfortunately, cannot automatically move from "could have" to "should have" to "would have" to "did," without specific evidence supporting such links. For the most enthusiastic embrace of the notion that the Nag Hammadi writings should be read (as a whole) as providing access to Jesus fully on a par with the canonical Gospels, see M. Franzmann, *Jesus in the Nag Hammadi Writings* (Edinburgh: T. & T. Clark, 1996).

28. See, for example, S. J. Patterson, *The Gospel of Thomas and Jesus* (Sonoma, Calif.: Polebridge Press, 1993); J. S. Kloppenborg, et al., *Q-Thomas Reader* (Sonoma, Calif.: Polebridge Press, 1990); R. Valantasis, *The Gospel of Thomas* (London: Routledge, 1997). This approach has been exploited most fully by Funk in *The Five Gospels* and by Crossan in *The Historical Jesus*.

Help also seemed to be available from the use of social scientific models applied to the first-century Mediterranean world.[30] Once more, however, no matter how theoretically interesting, models are only as good as the data to which they are applied. They cannot by themselves supply the deficiencies in specific information.[31] Thus, even if we were to grant the accuracy of the category "Peasant"

---

29. Caution concerning the overly optimistic use of *Gospel of Thomas* as a source for the historical Jesus derives from four considerations. First, the possibility that the sayings in the *Gospel of Thomas* resembling those in the canonical Gospels are in some fashion dependent on them cannot easily be dismissed. Among studies holding out this possibility are R. McL. Wilson, *Studies in the Gospel of Thomas* (London: Mowbray, 1960); B. Gaertner, *The Theology of the Gospel of Thomas*, trans. E. Sharpe (London: Collins, 1961); F. M. Strickert, "The Pronouncement Sayings in the Gospel of Thomas and the Synoptics," diss., University of Iowa, 1988; J.-E. Menard, *L'Evangile selon Thomas*, Nag Hammadi Studies 5 (Leiden: Brill, 1975); W. Schrage, *Das Verhaltnis des Thomas-Evangeliums zur synoptischen Tradition und zu koptischen Evangelienuebersetzungen*, BZNW 29 (Berlin: A. Toepelmann, 1964); H. Montefiore and H. E. W. Turner, *Thomas and the Evangelists* (London: SCM Press, 1962). A particularly discerning analysis is provided by Meier, *A Marginal Jew*, 1:123–39. Second, an adequate account of the *Gospel of Thomas* as a whole must take into consideration not only the links with the canonical tradition but also those with the larger Nag Hammadi corpus. For example, *Gospel of Thomas* 75 and 104 speak of a "Bridal Chamber," a phrase that finds contextualization in the *Gospel of Philip* 75:25–76:5; likewise, the woman with the "broken jar" in *Gospel of Thomas* 97 finds its most compelling contextualization in *Gospel of Truth* 26:4–25. Third, the issue of *Gospel of Thomas* and the canonical gospels must take into account the clear evidence that many of the other Nag Hammadi writings make use of the canonical literature (see C. M. Tuckett, *Nag Hammadi and the Gospel Tradition*, ed. J. Riches [Edinburgh: T. & T. Clark, 1986]). Fourth, the methods of determining layers of redaction must, in any case, be subjected to the most serious scrutiny because of their inevitable circularity; see C. M. Tuckett, "Q and Thomas: Evidence of a Primitive 'Wisdom Gospel'? A Response to H. Koester," *Ephemerides Theologicae Lovanienses* 67 (1991): 346–60.

30. J. M. Robinson considered a "new concept of history and the self" as a reason for legitimating a new quest after the failure of the old. What he meant, however, was a highly theologized attempt to discover the church's *kerygma* in the sayings of Jesus as revelatory of his "self-understanding." The results of this approach are shown most dramatically in G. Bornkamm's *Jesus of Nazareth*, trans. I. and F. McLuskey (New York: Harper and Row, 1960). The new quest, in contrast, makes explicit use of social-scientific models as a means of arguing by analogy and of amplifying and clarifying the sparse data from antiquity. For the general perspective of this approach, see B. Malina, *The New Testament World: Insights from Cultural Anthropology*, rev. ed. (Louisville, Ky.: Westminster/John Knox Press, 1993), and R. Rohrbaugh, ed., *The Social Sciences and New Testament Interpretation* (Peabody, Mass.: Hendrickson, 1996). For the use of such models, see especially Crossan's use of Harold Lenski's class analysis in *The Historical Jesus*, 43–46.

as applied to Jesus,[32] the classification is of limited use in determining what a specific historical person so designated could or could not have done or thought in that world.[33]

Finally, many scholars trained in the methods of source and form criticism had become convinced that by means of stylistic and thematic analysis they could discriminate between layers of redaction within a single composition and, on that basis, virtually "discover" new sources within old ones.[34] Paying little heed to those who thought such methods highly subjective and arbitrary, they considered themselves to have found the alchemist's stone that could finally break through the barrier that had stymied the earlier quest:[35] they could sort through the various strands of discrete tradition and find those that went back to Jesus himself as opposed to those that betrayed the influence of the early church.[36] New information, new models, and new methods encouraged the new questers, who believed that their efforts would yield more scientifically respectable results.[37]

---

31. See, e.g., the way in which theory tends to trump evidence in W. R. Herzog, *Parables as Subversive: Jesus as Pedagogue of the Oppressed* (Louisville, Ky.: Westminster/John Knox Press, 1994).

32. See Crossan, *The Historical Jesus*, 45–46, 124–36; In contrast, Meier provides nuanced comments on the difficulty of sorting out Jesus' precise socioeconomic status in *A Marginal Jew* 1:278–315.

33. Two observations are in order. The first is that the Roman empire was, in truth, a highly stratified social system, but it was equally one of social mobility and change (see W. A. Meeks, *The First Urban Christians: The Social World of the Apostle Paul* [New Haven: Yale University Press, 1983]). The second is that even in stratified worlds, the performance of individuals is distinctive and cannot be deduced from the supposed norm. Crossan himself notes the pertinence of Petronius' character Trimalchio (*The Historical Jesus*, 53–58).

34. Source criticism, form criticism, and redaction criticism are all variations of the same sort of diachronic approach that was formerly called "literary criticism," namely, the effort to create a historical sequence out of extant literary compositions by means of literary detection. For an accessible survey of such approaches, see S. L. McKenzie and S. R. Haynes, *To Each Its Own Meaning: An Introduction to Biblical Criticisms and Their Application* (Louisville, Ky.: Westminster/John Knox Press, 1993), 29–99. Such procedures operate on the premise that literary "seams" (changes in vocabulary, perspective, theme) are invariably indicators of "sources" that have been stitched together over the process of time rather than rhetorically shaped "signals" within the composition itself. The detection of "layers" is usually based on the premise that distinguishable ideological strands are incapable of being held simultaneously. Thus, both Bultmann and the Jesus Seminar insist that "sapiential" and "eschatological" elements within the gospels (or Q) must come from different periods of time, even though there are extant noncanonical writings (e.g. the *Testaments of the Twelve Patriarchs*) in which they comfortably coexist.

By 1999, however, it has become abundantly clear that these hopes are not to be realized, and that the old circularity, far from being transcended, is only more obvious. It is surely not entirely a coincidence that liberally inclined academics of the late twentieth century have found a Jesus who is not embarrassingly eschatological, not especially Jewish, not offensively religious, a canny crafter of countercultural aphorisms who is multicultural, egalitarian, an advocate of open commensality, and a reformer who is against the exclusive politics of holiness and for the inclusive politics of compassion. And best of all, he is all this as a charismatic peasant whose wisdom is not spoiled by literacy.[38] What more perfect mirror of late-twentieth-century academic social values and professional self-despising could be imagined? Nor is it surprising that at the opposite end of the cultural and religious spectrum, more evangelically oriented Christians are finding a Jesus who is precisely eschatological, devoted to purity and holiness, and a champion of the politics of restoration within Judaism.[39] Clearly, scholars' preunderstanding of Jesus deeply affects their way of assessing the data.[40]

---

35. The quest described by Schweitzer was in reality the pursuit of the literary composition that gave best access to Jesus. When Markan priority had been established, then it seemed imperative either to accept its portrayal of Jesus as an eschatologically motivated prophet, or to challenge its historical accuracy. The new quest follows on the challenge to Mark by Wilhelm Wrede that led to the development of form criticism. All of the gospels (including the *Gospel of Thomas*) are taken as theological constructions by the evangelists—the task of the historian is to assess the pieces used by each evangelist.

36. There is a direct line of continuity here between the methodological principles of the very conservative Joachim Jeremias in *The Parables of Jesus* and those employed by the Jesus Seminar in *The Five Gospels*. The gospels are seen as fundamentally distorting the memory of what Jesus said; in order to get back to the "real Jesus," one must peel away those parts of the gospel that reflect the tradition's perspective. What in Luther had been an appeal to the gospels against the tradition of Catholicism became in critical scholarship an appeal to Jesus against all tradition. What has characterized the new quest is that this opposition is carried to the gospel narratives themselves. The only sources available for learning about Jesus are themselves fundamentally unreliable in what they report about Jesus.

37. Although not formally associated with the Jesus Seminar, the work of Burton Mack shares the same methodological assumptions and, in the analysis of the hypothetical document Q, posits an earliest stratum of Jesus traditions that are fundamentally sapiential in character, unaffected by eschatology; see B. Mack, *The Lost Gospel: The Book of Q and Christian Origins* (San Francisco: HarperSanFrancisco, 1993), and my comments in *The Real Jesus*, 50–54.

38. This portrait is an amalgam of those in Crossan, *The Historical Jesus*; Borg, *Jesus, a New Vision*; and Funk, *Honest to Jesus*.

If neither the intrinsic interest of the subject matter nor the possibility for success accounts for the perpetuation of the quest for the historical Jesus, then perhaps the searchers are driven by some sense of compulsion. They work at this difficult and discouraging task out of a sense of necessity. To turn it another way, they will not give up on this task, no matter what its odd permutations, for to give it up would mean to lose something of essential value. This conclusion makes a lot of sense to me and corresponds to the almost fierce dedication I sense in conversation with questers, a devotion that survives any criticism of their perspectives, procedures, or results.[41]

It is tempting to attribute such a futile expenditure of time and energy to nonintellectual motives. It may be that the compulsion in some cases is economic and professional. Scholars need to publish to keep their jobs. And publishers have found that nothing in the field of religion sells like Jesus books. Those who have been educated only within these methods and know how to pursue only this one task are likely to keep publishing in it and are likely to find ready outlets for their productions, no matter how much the entire enterprise is challenged.[42]

The compulsion may, in some cases, also be deeply personal. Is it accidental that many contemporary questers were raised in a fundamentalist context that demanded an unswerving loyalty to the "literal" meaning of the text in support of doctrine?[43] For some, the pursuit of critical scholarship has literally been a conversion to another faith system. The freedom given by the doctrines and practices of scholarship offers salvation from the bondage to the literalism

---

39. See the portraits drawn by Sanders, *Jesus and Judaism;* Wright, *Jesus and the Victory of God*; and B. Chilton, *Pure Kingdom: Jesus' Vision of God* (Grand Rapids, Mich.: Eerdmans, 1996).

40. Robert Funk is simply the most transparent example. In his opening address to the newly formed Jesus Seminar in 1985, Funk already enunciated the image of Jesus that was required (see *Forum* 1, no. 1 [1985]: 10–12). It is no surprise, then, to find precisely that Jesus "determined" by the votes of the Seminar in *The Five Gospels* (1993). But the degree to which Funk was willing to ignore the very criteria established by the Seminar in order to "find" the Jesus he desired only became apparent in *Honest to Jesus*, 143–216.

41. In the various debates and discussions I have had with questers after the publication of *The Real Jesus*, I have been struck by the elusiveness of the conversation. When I challenged the quest on the grounds of historical method, the response tended to be in terms of the theological legitimacy of the quest; when I challenged the theological premises on the basis of classic Christian belief, the response tended to be in terms of historiography. For a sample, see the published form of the exchange at the 1996 AAR/SBL meeting, in C. A. Evans, A. Y. Collins, W. Wink, and L. T. Johnson, "The 'Real Jesus' in Debate," *Bulletin for Biblical Research* 7 (1997): 225–54.

of a narrowly defined tradition. But a world defined by literalism is difficult to escape. Repulsed by the Jesus they associate with their own oppressive rearing, some still cannot break free of Jesus or of the texts of oppression and must spend their lives, like obsessives unable to get past a primordial trauma, walking the same small circle again and again.[44]

Such explanations clearly do not, however, apply to all those engaged in historical Jesus research,[45] and I raise them only to say that even if such motivations were at work it would still be necessary to consider the overt reasons given (when they are given) for engaging in this search. And it is to these overt—if often unexpressed—motivations that I now turn.

In one way or another, the quest of the historical Jesus appears to rest upon the twofold conviction that (a) the humanity of Jesus is important, indeed, essential for Christians to maintain and (b) historical knowledge is the best way to apprehend Jesus' humanity. If this is so, then it is pertinent to inquire more persistently and precisely into this conviction. In the remainder of this chapter, I will consider some of its possible permutations, asking whether the double premise of the questers is, in fact, either necessary or correct.

At the most basic level, it might be argued, the historical study of Jesus is required in order to ensure that Christianity is not based simply in myth. Thus, if we can show that Jesus was a Jew of the first century, then he can be called "real" in the sense that Socrates is real, as opposed to, let us say, Osiris

---

42. Statements such as this one are guaranteed to generate resentment, as I discovered in responses to the observation in *The Real Jesus* 2–3, that the members of the Jesus Seminar were not drawn from the most notable research institutions in the United States. My statement was taken by readers as elitist, when in fact it was intended as the most sober sort of qualification of the Seminar's own posture as representing the best in critical scholarship. Therefore, I want to stress here that I am not, in making the observation in the text, questioning either the intellectual ability or the moral integrity of questers. I am rather asserting something important about the shape of New Testament scholarship today. The proliferation of the premises and procedures exemplified in the search for the historical Jesus points to a crisis in biblical scholarship that I try to address in *The Real Jesus*, 57–80.

43. To some extent at least this must account for the scarcely controlled rage against "Televangelists" and "Fundamentalists" expressed, for example, by *The Five Gospels*, 1–35, and J. S. Spong, *Born of a Woman*, 1–14—and more or less equated with "creedal Christianity."

44. This impression is most vivid in R. Funk's *Honest to Jesus*, in which Funk's personal story, reconstruction of Jesus, and vision for Christianity connect in the theme of "leavetaking and homecoming."

45. Indeed, the monumental research of Meier, *A Marginal Jew*, seems to be singularly lacking in such factors.

or Attis, namely, the religious figuration of natural processes. Jesus cannot thereby be reduced either to a societal ideal or mass neurosis. This is certainly a legitimate aim. But several observations are in order.

The first observation is that securing this much historicity is extraordinarily easy. Only the truly eccentric mind can fail to draw the appropriate conclusion from the available evidence, namely, that Christianity is linked to a Jew who was legally executed under Roman authority.[46] Establishing that much historicity is a half hour's work. It does not account for the extraordinary efforts of the Jesus questers.

The second observation is that the history-versus-myth distinction is itself a bit dangerous, if it is then taken as equaling "real" versus "unreal."[47] A more sophisticated sense of myth recognizes that the mythic is language seeking to express a depth of meaning that transcends the categories of analysis. In this sense, the statement "God is at work in history" is as surely mythic as is the statement "God was at work in Jesus." If history demands that the subject studied be reduced entirely to its categories of cognition, then history must disallow all religious language.[48]

Another motivation for pursuing the historical Jesus is to save Christianity from docetism. Docetism refers to the conviction among some early Christians, particularly the Gnostics, that Jesus' humanity was not real but only an appearance; the divine word simply inhabited some available human flesh in its sojourn on earth.[49] This is in reality a variation of the previous motivation,

---

46. An outstanding example of such a mind is J. M. Allegro, *The Sacred Mushroom and the Cross: A Study of the Nature and Origins of Christianity within the Fertility Cults of the Near East* (London: Hodder and Stoughton, 1970). The title pretty much says it all.

47. It was precisely this easy and deceptive equation that led to my (ironic) title, *The Real Jesus*. John Meier makes important distinctions between the "reality" of any figure of the past and the limited capabilities of any historical reconstruction; see *A Marginal Jew* 1:21–40; 2:340, 682, 778.

48. For a (not entirely satisfactory) response to this premise, see C. S. Evans, *The Historical Christ and the Jesus of Faith: The Incarnational Narrative as History* (Oxford: Clarendon Press, 1996).

49. The claim that the quest for the historical Jesus was necessary as a protection against docetism was made explicitly by J. D. Crossan in the first of his entries in the Spring 1996 Internet debate sponsored by HarperSanFrancisco and involving Crossan, Borg, and myself ("Jesus2000"). Crossan claimed that my strong position concerning the resurrection as the basis of Christian faith was in effect a variation of Gnosticism. I found this a classic example of historical reductionism, in which a theological conviction concerning the humanity of Jesus (which I strongly affirm) is identified with a process of historical reconstruction (which I strongly reject as the appropriate path to that humanity).

except that it involves an explicitly theological concern. Whether Jesus' humanity was real or not, a divine artifice is of no concern to the secular historian, who is content if Christianity is based on illusion. Still less should a secular historian worry if what Christians proclaimed about Jesus was not in continuity with what Jesus himself proclaimed.[50] Such concerns derive from a faith commitment that makes the human figure of Jesus the measure for Christian confession.

Again, some observations are in order. It is not at all clear, in the first place, that if Jesus' humanity *were* docetic, history would be in a position to detect it, since history, like all empirical disciplines, depends entirely on the observation and analysis of phenomena. It cannot declare on the ontic status of things, only on their appearance; history gives no access to the noumenal. And since history can only negotiate that set of "appearances" of Jesus recorded in the gospels, it is not able to declare whether those appearances were of a "real human" or only of an "apparent human." This motivation for doing historical Jesus research is also somewhat odd in that it is based on the same sort of creedal premise that questers frequently castigate for "theological tyranny" and the suppression of the historical Jesus. Here is a case where the creed seems to give even as it takes away.

But is the charge accurate in the first place? Does the Christian creed actually diminish the humanity of Jesus? Certainly it does not do so explicitly. The Nicene Creed, for example, declares that Jesus was "conceived of the Holy Spirit, born of the virgin Mary, suffered under Pontius Pilate, was crucified, died and was buried." The only transcendental element in this summary is the mode of conception by the Holy Spirit. That Jesus was conceived, however, and born of a specific woman, suffered, and died a form of violent execution under a specific historically locatable Roman prefect, and finally was buried— these seem to stress rather than diminish Jesus' humanity.[51]

Perhaps, however, I am being overly literal. Perhaps the real complaint about the creed or "Creedal Christians" is that, despite their protestations to

---

50. This is a concern especially of the Second Quest, associated with Ernst Käsemann, who stated candidly, "The clash over the historical Jesus has as its object a genuine theological problem" ("The Problem of the Historical Jesus," 34), which he identifies as "enthusiasm," or the tendency of a resurrection faith to dissolve the preached Christ "into the projection of an eschatological self-consciousness and becoming the object of a religious ideology" ("Blind Alleys," 63). For Käsemann, therefore, the quest for the historical Jesus was the quest for "criteria" as a "discerning of the spirits" ("Blind Alleys," 48), namely, to discover "whether the earthly Jesus is to be taken as the criterion of the kerygma, and if so, to what extent" ("Blind Alleys," 47). For this aspect of Käsemann's work, see B. Ehler, *Die Herrschaft des Gekreuzigten*, BZNW 46 (Berlin: DeGruyter, 1986), 161–269.

the contrary, their explicit conviction concerning Jesus' divine nature, or their conviction that he continues to live as the resurrected one as life-giving Spirit, means that *in effect* his humanity is not taken sufficiently seriously: Jesus' humanity is just a sort of abstract proposition, without any specificity.

Is this claim true? Have creedal Christians made the humanity of Jesus a mere cipher? The evidence, I suggest, is mixed. There is considerable evidence that the humanity of Jesus receives scant attention in much contemporary Christian preaching, especially the forms that portray Christian existence not as a path of discipleship in the way of the cross, but purely as a salvation from psychic troubles and a placement on the path to worldly success. Indeed, the lack of attention to the humanity of Jesus in the church is in all likelihood the strongest element in the popularity of current historical Jesus research. People are eager to hear about the person of Jesus of Nazareth and do not hear about him often enough within the community of faith.

But it should also be emphasized that such neglect is not the necessary corollary of a creedal faith. Here is where the easy equation between creedal Christianity and "fundamentalism" and "literalism" becomes most obviously distorting. The very same patristic theologians who spun such fine distinctions concerning Nature and Person preached sermons that meditated on the gospels in great and specific detail. To take but one example, hear this Christmas sermon from Leo the Great. After speaking of Jesus' humility and service to humans, Leo concludes:

> These works of our Lord, dearly beloved, are useful to us, not only for their communication of grace, but as an example for our imitation also—if only these remedies would be turned into instruction, and what has been bestowed by the mysteries would benefit the way people live. Let us remember that we must live in the "humility and meekness" of our Redeemer, since, as the Apostle says, "if we suffer with him, we shall also reign with him." In vain are we called Christians if we do not imitate Christ. For this reason did he refer to himself as the Way, that the teacher's manner of life might be the exemplar for his disciples, and that the servant might choose the humility which had been practiced by the master, who lives and reigns forever and ever. Amen.[52]

---

51. Not least because the creed, as a *regula fidei* drawn from the canonical scriptures themselves, points to the fuller narrative expression of these convictions in the New Testament gospels and letters. It is certainly true that these notes on Jesus' humanity are preceded and followed by thoroughly mythic claims concerning his ultimate origin in God and his future role as judge of humanity, but these contextualize Jesus' humanity rather than suppress it.

And if the high Middle Ages can be called the apex of abstract and propositional theology, it can also legitimately be called an age of unparalleled devotion to the humanity of Jesus in prayer, meditation, music, and art.[53] The frescoes of Giotto were not made by someone unappreciative of Jesus' humanity.

But such attention to Jesus' humanity within the tradition, it may be claimed, focuses on his universal human characteristics rather than the historical particularities of his time and place. Most specifically, some object, it is the Jewishness of Jesus that creedal Christianity suppresses.[54] Before taking up this issue, it should be recognized that the ground of objection has shifted once more. Not simply the humanity of Jesus but *what aspect* of his humanity is now at question. The ancient church focused on the character of Jesus as exemplary of virtue. Contemporary questers focus on his social and ideological location in antiquity as a Jew. It is not immediately obvious, however, why one focus is more serious about Jesus' humanity than the other.

Why should Jesus' *Jewishness* be of such signal importance apart from specific theological convictions concerning special revelation within Israel? The obvious answer is that in a post-Holocaust world the neglect of Jesus' Jewishness is considered as fundamental to the long and tragic story of Christian anti-Semitism.[55] And it is certainly true that, to the degree Jesus' humanity has either been subsumed into his status as God's Son or has been abstracted from his Jewish identity, Christians have found it easier to distance themselves from and stand in hostile opposition to Judaism. For these reasons, all of the historical data concerning Judaism in the first century which has become available within the past forty years has had the most positive effect in contextualizing Jesus, the nascent Christian movement, and the very language

---

52. See Leo the Great, *Sermon* 25:5–6 (25 December 444); citation from St. Leo the Great, *Sermons*, trans. J. P. Freeland and A. J. Conway, The Fathers of the Church 93 (Washington D.C.: Catholic University of America Press, 1996), 103–4. See also *Sermon* 37:3–4; 46:2–3; 59:4–5; 66:4–5; 70:4–5; 72:4–5; likewise, Caesarius of Arles, *Sermon* 11; Jerome, *Homily* 88; Origen, *Homilies on Luke* 20:5; 29:5–7; 34; 38:1–3.

53. Among countless examples, see Thomas à Kempis, *Imitation of Christ* 4:7–12; Bernard of Clairvaux, *On the Song of Songs,* Sermon 20; Francis of Assisi, *Rule of 1221,* chaps. 1–2, 9; see also Caroline Walker Bynum, *Jesus as Mother: Studies in the Spirituality of the High Middle Ages* (Berkeley: University of California Press, 1982).

54. See in particular G. Vermes, *Jesus the Jew*, 15–17, and *Jesus and the World of Judaism*, 49–51.

55. See, e.g., R. Ruether, *Faith and Fratricide: The Theological Roots of Anti-Semitism* (New York: Seabury, 1974); A. R. Eckhardt, *Jews and Christians: The Contemporary Meeting* (Bloomington: Indiana University Press, 1986). The concern is explicit in Crossan's *Who Killed Jesus.*

of the New Testament. Like all other critical scholars, I affirm the absolute necessity of learning as much about the historical circumstances of the New Testament as possible in order to understand its symbolic structure and its claims.[56] Not least among the values of such historical study is the relativization of the rhetoric of the New Testament concerning the Jews.[57]

The pursuit of historical knowledge in order to place the New Testament in context is not the same thing, however, as pursuing a historical reconstruction of the figure of Jesus. As I mentioned earlier, none of the new knowledge (or re-examined old knowledge) concerning Judaism in the first century appears to touch directly on Jesus himself. The primary result of this knowledge is to increase our sense of the complexity of Jewish life both in Palestine and in the Diaspora, and to engender a sense of caution about simple declarations concerning what it meant to be a Jew.[58] To construct a single narrative or portrait of Judaism in first-century Palestine is to distort the evidence of history.[59]

A further historical distortion occurs when a single strand within the complex world of Judaism is isolated and stabilized (or, one might say, hypostatized) in order to provide a coherent framework to place the Jesus traditions salvaged from the deconstructed gospel narratives. This is, in fact, what is done in several recent historical Jesus publications: Judaism is used to provide a norm against which to measure Jesus.[60] Such studies claim to root Jesus in Judaism, but in reality one or the other aspect of that complex and living tradition is singled out and reified as a category into which Jesus can be placed. He is a charismatic Jew, or an eschatological Jew, or a Jewish peasant.

---

56. See L. T. Johnson, *The Writings of the New Testament: An Interpretation* (Philadelphia: Fortress Press, 1986), especially the introduction and epilogue.

57. These convictions are displayed in a number of my own writings, including "The New Testament's Anti-Jewish Slander and the Conventions of Ancient Polemic," *Journal of Biblical Literature* 108 (1989): 419–41, and "Religious Rights and Christian Texts," in *Religious Human Rights in Global Perspective*, ed. J. Witte and J. D. van de Vyver, 2 vols. (The Hague: Martinus Nijhoff, 1996), 1:65–95.

58. See Johnson, "New Testament's Anti-Jewish Slander," 423–30.

59. This is the major flaw in the otherwise impressive effort of N. T. Wright, *Christian Origins and the Question of God*, vol. 1, *The New Testament and the People of God* (London: SPCK, 1992). His concern to construct a single narrative framework leads to a tendency to speak in terms of "mainline Jews" (see p. 286), in much the same manner as G. F. Moore spoke of "Normative Judaism" (in his *Judaism in the First Centuries of the Christian Era*, 2 vols. [1927; New York: Schocken Books, 1971]).

60. In a 1987 lecture called "Jesus within Judaism" at Christian Theological Seminary in Indianapolis, I demonstrated this tendency in H. Falk, *Jesus the Pharisee: A New Look at the Jewishness of Jesus* (New York: Paulist Press, 1985); Vermes, *Jesus the Jew*; and Sanders, *Jesus and Judaism*.

Such categories, in turn, are used as boundaries to what Jesus could and could not have done as a human person. A charismatic Jew would not be interested in observance of the law, an apocalyptic Jew must have been committed to the restoration of the temple, a peasant Jew could not read and write. But history has to do precisely with the way actual living people in the past have drawn attention to themselves for the strange and wondrous ways in which they have confounded their settings and conditioning. Julius Caesar is not every Roman, nor is Socrates every Athenian. To reduce Jesus' possibilities to what was available to a hypothetical Jewish construct is not to do history but to engage in sociological typecasting. So much does recent historical reconstruction tend to stabilize and hypostatize fluid and complex traditions in the service of "finding" a specific and comprehensible Jesus, in fact, that I propose reversing the charge that the questers customarily make against the tradition: Do they not end up being just as abstract as the creeds of Christianity ever were?

The final motivation for Jesus research is the conviction that Jesus' humanity is in some fashion or other normative for Christian identity. There are three different ways of articulating this conviction. Two of them lead to some sort of historical reconstruction. The third does not.

The first way to express this has been the most consistent within historical Jesus research from Reimarus to Robert Funk.[61] It begins with a triple conviction: first, that Christianity is not a uniquely or divinely revealed truth but is rather, like all religions, a cultural construction elastic in its capacity to reinvent itself; second, that Christianity in its present state distorts its important humane values by various forms of superstition, beginning with the notion of divine revelation; third, that as the central symbol of Christianity, Jesus must be the repository of the positive humane values without the distortions of supernatural claptrap.[62]

The quest for a purely human Jesus is, then, the search for a purely human Christianity, the desire for a Jesus without dogma is a desire for Christianity without dogma, the conviction that Jesus must have been a simple moral teacher a reflection of the conviction that Christianity ought to be a matter of simple morality without sacrament or institutional superstructure.[63]

Questers of this sort suffer the agonies of unrecognized reformers and prophets. They can't stand the Christianity practiced in the churches, but can't

---

61. See Allen, *The Human Christ*, 92–119.

62. See Funk, *Honest to Jesus*, 300–314; see also the final sentence in Crossan's *The Historical Jesus*, "If you cannot believe in something produced by reconstruction, you may have nothing left to believe in" (426).

63. See Crossan, *The Historical Jesus*, 417–26.

stand to leave it either; they regard the Jesus portrayed in the gospels as corrupted as the Jesus preached from the pulpit, but they cannot imagine their lives without reference to Jesus. Most of all, they cannot understand why other Christians do not want to accept the liberation they offer.[64] Their solution is to craft a Jesus who suits their sense of what Christianity ought to be. And since images of an ideal Christianity differ according to personal perspective, so do such questers come up with the bewildering variety of "historical" Jesuses that I have catalogued above. The most recent versions clearly represent a reaction against the supposed individualism and otherworldliness of present Christianity; thus, in one way or another, Jesus and his mission are defined in social or political rather than in religious or spiritual terms.[65]

The second articulation of the conviction that Jesus' humanity is normative for Christians is the conviction that what Jesus said and did before his death, indeed his vision of reality, is normative for Christians because in those words and actions and perceptions God was expressing the norm for human life. This is, in effect, a way of expressing the doctrine of the incarnation. The resurrection of Jesus only validated what was there all along but could not be seen: that Jesus was the unique revelation of God.[66] A traditional enough understanding in many ways—why should it demand a historical reconstruction?

It does so if the gospels are taken as inadequate historical sources for the "real Jesus" rather than as witnesses and interpretations of him in the light of faith. If the way to get at what God was expressing in Jesus demands "getting behind" the gospels, in order to reach that elusive human person in whom was embodied revelation, then some sort of sifting and rearranging of the gospel materials seems to be required. The theological character of this motivation is immediately apparent. History is put in service of the search for a pure revelation that

---

64. Funk, *Honest to Jesus*, 11–14.

65. The sort of sociopolitical renderings of Jesus offered by Borg and Crossan need to be challenged historiographically in terms of the adequacy of the portrayal of the historical/social situation and the selection of the evidence from the gospels. But in terms of their theological agenda, such reconstructions can be challenged as well on two counts: (1) Their tendency to reify Judaism and—contrary to their good intentions—perpetuate the picture of a good Jesus (for a politics of compassion/unbrokered kingdom against a bad Judaism (which has a politics of holiness or participates in a brokered kingdom). This is a mild form of the Marcionism that has long infected forms of Christianity that focus on what is unique about Christianity/Jesus as what is essential to Jesus/Christianity. (2) Their reduction of religious sensibility to the level of political position, which represents an impoverished view of reality, not to mention traditional Christianity, which has based itself on the conviction that Jesus was less about the rearrangement of the structures of society than the transformation of the very structures of existence.

is all the more mythic because it is presumed to be available somewhere beyond the contingent perspectives of the sources.

What is most paradoxical here, however, is the fusion of the contingent and the necessary. History has to do with the contingent, the singular, and the unrepeatable. In what sense can the "history" of Jesus—the specifics of his place and time and words and gestures—be normative? How can these serve, that is, as a necessary frame of reference for all other "histories," in the lives of those who live in quite different times and places, and who must interact with quite different circumstances, who must speak with different words and who must act with different gestures? This is, at root, the mystery of the incarnation, that Kierkegaard recognized as the absurd yet compelling conjunction of the necessary (eternal) and contingent (temporal).[67] Christians claim that in the contingent events of Jesus' life, the "eternal" of God is revealed, yes. But it is not possible for the specifics of any (unrepeatable) human existence to be normative for others—by definition.

If the historical is to bear normativity, must it not be through some pattern found in the person of the past which is in fact applicable to all others? Here is the failure in logic in the well-meaning efforts of those believers who are also questers.[68]

Marcus Borg says, "To follow Jesus means in some sense to be 'like him,' to take seriously what he took seriously," which, he proposes, gives disciples

---

66. Ernst Käsemann ("Blind Alleys," 27, 29, 31) quotes Joachim Jeremias ("The Present Position in the Controversy Concerning the Problem of the Historical Jesus," *Expository Times* 69 [1958]: 333–39] to this effect: "The Incarnation implies that Jesus is not only a possible subject for historical research, study, and criticism, but that it demands all of these… according to the New Testament, there is no other revelation of God but the Incarnate Word.… The Historical Jesus and His message are not one presupposition among many for the kerygma, but the sole presupposition of the kerygma"; the quest for the historical Jesus is therefore the gaining of revelation: "we can venture on [this road] with confidence, nor need we fear that we are embarking on a perilous, fruitless adventure." Compare N. T. Wright, "A truly first-century Jewish theological perspective would teach us to recognize that history, especially the history of first-century Judaism, is the sphere where we find, at work to judge and to save, the God who made the world" (*Jesus and the Victory of God*, 662).

67. S. Kierkegaard, *Concluding Unscientific Postscript,* trans. D. F. Swenson and W. Lowrie (Princeton: Princeton University Press, 1944), 498–515. I recognize that my use of the "eternal" here is not the same as Kierkegaard's.

68. It is also, of course, the failure of arguments such as those used to support the exclusion of women from ordained ministry on the grounds that Jesus and the apostles were male. The same logic could be extended to demand that all priests be Jewish, wear beards, and live in Palestine.

"an alternative vision of life."[69] He is partly right: to be a disciple must be to be like Jesus in some fashion, and that means having a different vision. But he is, I think, seriously in error when he explicates that as "taking seriously what he took seriously," for it defines the pattern and vision in terms of the specific historical circumstances of Jesus' unrepeatable life, which are not only largely unrecoverable but also largely irrelevant.[70]

When Borg goes on to characterize Jesus' historical mission as one in which he opposed the "politics of holiness" that dominated Judaism with a "politics of compassion," he ends up with what turns out to be an abstract pattern that is applicable only to some humans in some circumstances. He is a bit like an engineer who tries to persuade us of the usefulness of bridges in general but is able to construct only a bridge capable of spanning one size river.

This brings us at last to the third way of thinking about Jesus' humanity as normative for all Christians, a way that characterized Christianity from the time of the writing of the New Testament to the period of the Enlightenment, when the quest for the historical Jesus began in Europe. This classical form of Christianity based itself on belief in the resurrection, which means that the response of faith is directed not to a set of facts about a man of the past who had died but to a person who had entered into the life of God so fully that he continues to be present as life-giving spirit.[71]

It was this resurrection experience that shaped the church's memory of Jesus' words and deeds and that led it to understand the deeper dimensions of his humanity, so that it came to see that even before entering through death into his glory this human person carried the full weight of the divine presence and was the incarnate revelation of God.

Yet within the writings of the New Testament this resurrection faith did not translate into a denial or neglect of Jesus' humanity. Just the opposite. It

---

69. Borg, *Jesus, a New Vision*, 17.

70. Funk recognizes this when, after laboring to recover Jesus' distinctive vision of reality, he then adds, "To accept Jesus' sense of the real naively is also a potential mistake.... [W]e must test his perceptions of the real by our own extended and controlled observations on our world. We need not and should not place blind faith in what Jesus trusted." *Honest to Jesus,* 305.

71. See my *The Real Jesus,* 133–40, and *Writings of the New Testament* 1–20, 87–40, as well as my most recent book, *Living Jesus: Learning the Heart of the Gospel* (San Francisco: Harper SanFrancisco, 1999). The position I develop in *The Real Jesus* bears a real resemblance to the classic argument of Martin Kähler, *The So-Called Historical Jesus and the Historic, Biblical Christ,* trans. C. E. Braaten (1892; Philadelphia: Fortress Press, 1964), a point effectively made in a review of *The Real Jesus* by Sharon Dowd in *Lexington Theological Quarterly* 31, no. 2 (1996): 179–83.

deserves repetition that, apart from the pathetically few scraps of information about Jesus found in Greco-Roman and Jewish sources, absolutely everything we know about the human person Jesus—including every bit of data used by every so-called historical reconstruction of Jesus—derives from these believers who met and worshiped in the name of the living Lord and said Amen to God through him. This information is contained not only in the gospels but in the earliest Christian correspondence dating from as early as twenty years after Jesus' death: the letters of Paul, of Peter, and the anonymous Letter to the Hebrews all contain specific historical information about Jesus.[72]

It is above all, of course, the gospels that report on Jesus' deeds and words, with a specificity so detailed and acute that everything learned about Palestine in the past hundred years has served to support the portrait of life in that place found in the gospel narratives and the parables of Jesus.[73] Those who confessed Jesus as risen Lord can hardly be accused of neglecting his humanity if everything we know of his humanity derives from them!

At the same time, the New Testament writings and, above all, the gospels show no obsessive concern with an exhaustive record of Jesus' words and deeds, or even a preoccupation with getting the sequence of his deeds or the wording of his sayings perfectly accurate. This is so much the case that the entire quest for the historical Jesus has been confounded by the casualness of our primary sources on just these points.

There is one aspect of Jesus' humanity, however, on which the New Testament witnesses show remarkable unanimity, and that is Jesus' character, or what might be called the basic pattern of his life. They agree also that this pattern or character is also the norm for Jesus' followers.[74]

Notice the conceptual shift involved in recognizing this emphasis within the New Testament texts. To speak of character is to speak of persons—including historical persons—in a way that is different from that employed by historical Jesus researchers. According to questers at either end of the ideological spectrum, the person of Jesus can be located by the discovery of his authentic

---

72. For the information about the human Jesus found in the New Testament epistolary literature, see my *The Real Jesus*, 117–22, and more fully in *Living Jesus*.

73. This remarkable convergence and confirmation has held out the tantalizing prospect of being able to push even further, to Jesus himself, when in fact it only enables us to better grasp the literary presentation of Jesus within the Gospels with the sense that—despite their diversity—they construct a figure that all historical investigation shows to be thoroughly at home in that world.

74. My basic position here is in many ways similar to that of H. Frei, *The Identity of Jesus Christ: The Hermeneutical Bases of Dogmatic Theology* (Philadelphia: Fortress Press, 1975).

sayings, either apart from or in concert with his verifiable deeds. Each saying of Jesus, it is assumed, bears an "understanding of the world" or a "vision of reality" that either indicates or is constitutive of Jesus as a person. Likewise, each deed is an "enactment" of such a vision or understanding. Now, the importance of what people say and do should be obvious and can never be simply neglected. There is, therefore, a legitimacy to approaching the gospel materials with such an interest.

There is, however, the basic problem that an adequate inventory of Jesus' sayings and deeds is simply not available. And even if the ones made available to us in the sources were all tested and found to be authentic, they would represent a tiny portion of what Jesus spoke and did. More problematic still, however, is the premise that a person can be understood even if one were in possession of all the facts about them—all their words and all their deeds.

It is far more adequate generally to think of persons in terms of their character, that is, in terms of those traits, dispositions, attitudes, and habits that underlie, generate, and are articulated by specific deeds and sayings. To be a person is less a matter of event than of existence. To a considerable extent, a person's character is both what is most important about him or her—even historically—and what is often most elusive about him or her. The reason why "one's story" is thought to be particularly revealing of self is not because such reportage is necessarily more accurate or comprehensive on the facts, but because narrative necessarily involves an interpretation of the facts. The continuous writing of biographies about figures such as Thomas Jefferson and John F. Kennedy has less to do with the acquiring of new facts than with the need to assess character. And each new interpretation of character is accomplished by the placing of the "facts" into a different narrative.

Since the gospels were written from the perspective of faith in Jesus as the resurrected son of God, we might expect to find him consistently portrayed in the gospels as a triumphant, glorious figure. But the opposite is the case: Jesus is portrayed in the gospel narratives as the obedient one who gives his life in service for the sake of others, and who calls others to follow him in the same path of obedient service.[75] So much is this portrayal common to the four gospels that in other respects differ so greatly—even in the Gospel of John, in which the resurrection perspective is all pervasive—that literary critics have no difficulty in discerning the "Christ figure" in works of literature such as Melville's *Billy Budd* and Dostoevski's *The Idiot*. This figure is, of course, that of an innocent person whose suffering is redemptive for others.

---

75. See the development of this argument in *The Real Jesus*, 141–66, and in *Living Jesus*.

This portrayal of Jesus, I repeat, is found in the gospels, not in the individual sayings and stories but in their narrative shaping as such. It is an image of Jesus that is accessible not through historical analysis but through literary and religious apprehension.[76] The Jesus who moves through the pages of the canonical gospels can be located as a historical person of first-century Palestine, but his identity, his character as a human person, can be grasped only by grasping the literary presentation of him in these narratives.

More remarkably, this is also the character of Jesus found in Paul's letters, our earliest Christian writings. It is well known that Paul's appreciation of Jesus is entirely from the perspective of his resurrection; this is not surprising, since he did not know Jesus in his mortal life and encountered him first as powerful Lord mystically identified with the church Paul was persecuting. For Paul, then, Jesus is above all "Lord," the one before whom every knee should bow. But by no means does Paul reject the significance of Jesus' humanity.[77]

In his letters Paul reports very few words of Jesus, though when he does he regards them as authoritative (see 1 Cor. 7:10; 9:14; 11:23–25). And he tells no stories about Jesus' wonders.[78]

It appears that Paul is not primarily interested in telling the story of Jesus as a narrative about a figure of the past.[79] His passionate concern is for the process by which the Holy Spirit replicates the story of Jesus in believers' lives in the present. Those who live by the Spirit, he says, should also walk by the

---

76. See the helpful distinctions between the Jesus "of the text," "behind the text," and "before the text" in Sandra M. Schneiders, *The Revelatory Text: Interpreting the New Testament as Sacred Scripture* (San Francisco: HarperSanFrancisco, 1991), 97–179. I am speaking of the Jesus "of the text," as the one who is literarily accessible. The Jesus "before the text"—that is, the Jesus confessed as resurrected—is accessible through religious response. As I argue in *Living Jesus*, the construction of the living person who is Jesus involves a complex conversation between religious experience and literary texts among believers.

77. The exclusion of evidence from Paul as a possible control for the image of Jesus derived from the gospels is one of the most glaring ways in which much of the most recent quest for the historical Jesus reveals itself as driven by ideological as much as historical interests. To prefer the evidence from the (at best mid-second century) *Gospel of Thomas* to that available from our earliest datable witness to Jesus confounds all the rules of sober historiography.

78. This is not, as sometimes supposed, because Paul has an aversion for the miraculous; just the opposite: he repeatedly celebrates wonderworking in connection with the mission (1 Thess. 1:5; Gal. 3:5; 1 Cor. 2:2, 4:20; 2 Cor. 12:12; Rom. 15:18–19).

79. Although allusions like that in Gal. 3:1 remind us that Paul may well have told the story of Jesus' passion in his preaching.

Spirit (Gal. 5:25). And the Spirit's work is the transformation of humans into the new humanity created after the image of Jesus. Paul seeks to inculcate in his readers what he calls "the mind of Christ" (1 Cor. 2:16) or what he refers to in another place as "the law of Christ" (or perhaps better, the "Pattern of the Messiah"), which he spells out as "bear one another's burdens" (Gal. 6:2).[80] In his letter to the Philippians, Paul presents the "mind that was in Christ" as the model for his readers to follow as they "look not only to their own interests but also to the interests of others," namely, that attitude of Jesus which led him to liberate himself from the need to cling to his equality with God in order to devote himself utterly to humble obedience to God, even to his death on the cross.[81]

And repeatedly in his letters, Paul exhorts his readers to lives of self-donation for the building up of others, appealing as support for such behavior to the one "who loved me and gave himself for me" (Gal. 2:20). It is entirely fitting that one of the very few direct quotations of Jesus provided by Paul is the perfect expression of the pattern I have been describing in Jesus' own words:

> I received from the Lord what I also handed on to you, that the Lord Jesus on the night when he was betrayed took bread, and when he had given thanks, he broke it and said, "This is my body which is for you. Do this in remembrance of me." In the same way he took the cup, also after supper, saying, "This cup is the new covenant in my blood. Do this, as often as you drink it, in remembrance of me." (1 Cor. 11:23–25)[82]

The gospels and Paul—and, we could add, Peter and Hebrews also—remember as most important in Jesus his character, the way he disposed his freedom toward God and his fellow humans.[83] And this pattern of the Messiah, this

---

80. For the importance of an implied narrative about Jesus in the theology of Paul, see R. B. Hays, *The Faith of Jesus Christ: An Investigation of the Narrative Substructure of Galatians 3:1–4:11*, SBLDS 56 (Chico, Calif.: Scholars Press, 1983), and L. T. Johnson, *Reading Romans: A Literary and Theological Commentary* (New York: Crossroad Press, 1997).

81. See S. E. Fowl, *The Story of Christ in the Ethics of Paul: An Analysis of the Function of the Hymnic Material in the Pauline Corpus* (Sheffield: JSOT Press, 1990).

82. For discussion, see Johnson, *Religious Experience*.

83. For the discerning of this pattern in the other New Testament writings, see *Living Jesus*, and for the understanding of Jesus' freedom, see L. T. Johnson, *Faith's Freedom: A Classic Spirituality for Contemporary Christians* (Minneapolis: Fortress Press, 1991).

character of Jesus, was what they drew as normative for all those who sought to live by the Spirit of one who now shared God's own life. But in Paul and Peter and Hebrews, this character of Jesus, this pattern of a certain way of being human which serves as a model for other humans, is also not accessible to history, but must be apprehended literarily and religiously.

This is the understanding of Jesus' humanity that empowered and shaped the first Christians, and the image that continues to provide the norm for disciples. The character of Jesus in the gospels and in the letters of the New Testament is astonishingly vivid and unmistakable. It is available to every careful reader, even of the most meager education. It is embodied again and again in the lives of saints from Martin de Porres to Francis of Assisi to Dorothy Day to Mother Teresa, all of whom followed the path of loving service to the world's little ones in faithful obedience to God.

The quest for the historical Jesus—in all its permutations—has provided no image that matches this one in particularity or life. The main accomplishment of the quest, both early and late, has been the discrediting of the gospel portraits of Jesus, at an enormous cost. The alternatives offered by historical reconstruction reveal themselves as fantasies and abstractions, held together by scholarly cleverness, incapable of sustaining even close examination, much less of galvanizing human lives. The Jesus they present is a dead person of the past. For those, in contrast, whose lives are being transformed by the Spirit of the Living One, the Jesus depicted in the literary compositions of the New Testament is recognized as true, both to his life and to theirs.

3

The Quest for the Historical Jesus

From the Perspectives of Medieval, Modern, and Post-Enlightenment Readings, and in View of Ancient, Oral Aesthetics

Werner H. Kelber

But as the dialectic of the Enlightenment unfolded, it became trapped in ever narrower models of what could count as truth.

David Tracy

The force of fact as modernity has construed it has not gone uncontested.

Edith Wyschogrod

The best ethical criticism, ancient and modern, has insisted on the complexity and variety revealed to us in literature, appealing to that complexity to cast doubt on reductive theories.

Martha Nussbaum

Note: In writing this piece I have received valuable assistance from Professors Rachel Fulton, Gerald McKenny, Martha Nussbaum, Elaine Pagels, and above all from Edith Wyschogrod. Additionally, my students David A. Adcock and Robert N. Day have subjected the manuscript to an admirably critical reading. Furthermore, I express my respectful appreciation for the scholarly work of my colleagues in New Testament studies, Luke Timothy Johnson and John Dominic Crossan. Last but not least, I am grateful to Jens Schröter and his colleagues at the Institüt für Neues Testament, Universität Hamburg, for inviting me to deliver the German version of these lectures on June 1 and 3, 1999. To all my thanks.

By locating the world in relation to its creative origin we override the plurality and opacity of the world as phenomenologically accessible.

Joseph Stephen O'Leary

I have suggested that the non-scientific or protoscientific nature of historical studies is signaled in the inability of historians to agree—as the natural scientists of the seventeenth century were able to—on a specific mode of discourse.

Hayden White

The Early Church remains a period still charged with more than academic interest for many readers. Stereotypes, alternately placid and histrionic, gravitate around with remarkable ease.

Peter Brown

The Bible is the pivotal book in the Western tradition, and it is with us still, for good and ill.

If we try to appraise the Bible's impact purely in terms of its textual productivity, we will have to imagine an immense proliferation of biblical manuscripts both handwritten and typographically produced over centuries, including a polyphonic body of vernacular translations. By December 31, 1998, the Bible as a whole, Hebrew Bible plus New Testament, had been translated into 366 languages; and at least one book of the Bible had been translated and printed into 2,212 languages and dialects.[1] In addition, there exists a ceaseless and still expanding volume of commentaries and dictionaries, theological, literary, exegetical, and historical treatises on biblical books, themes, and characters. The Bible is a book overloaded with commentary. Imagining thus the Bible's generative powers, we gain a sense of the vast textual output still in progress and as yet unquenched that may be the most gigantic textual labor ever expended on a single book in the Western tradition. Lest we think of the impact of the Bible exclusively in textual, scriptural terms, we need to remember also its oral implementation, for it was mostly by way of oral recitation and homiletical exposition that the sacred scripture reached the people, teaching and converting, humbling and empowering them, and ministering to their spiritual and social needs. Listen also to music and its expressive transposition of biblical themes and stories into hymns and oratorios, liturgies and canticles, ranging from sensuously mystical simplicity to breathtaking virtuosity. And there are

---

1. This information was obtained in March 1999 from the American Bible Society.

the visual arts representing the grand themes of creation and judgment, exodus and last supper, the sacrifice (or binding) of Isaac and the annunciation, uncommon births and the crucifixion, and memorable characters such as Adam and Eve, David and Moses, the Madonna with the Child, Abraham and Jesus, Ruth and the woman who anointed Jesus, and countless others who have enriched the imagination of generations of viewers.

It is from the Hebrew Bible—alongside other books—that we inherited a sense of history—straining against eternal patterns of nature mythology and squarely placing human affairs at center stage. And it is from the Bible in its Hebrew and Christian versions that we derived a sense of what defines us and our place in history. Modeled after the image of God, and aspiring to glimpses of epiphany, humanity nonetheless is situated east of Eden and conscripted into the hard labor of civilization. This dual legacy bears down on the individual who is haunted by the fear of loss, yet endowed with redemptive potentials. History is textured with causal connectives and fractured expectations, and in this mingling of the realistic with the surprising it is always related back to the will of a God who manifests himself arrestingly immediate and direct, as well as uncannily inscrutable, acting out of a surplus of mercy, mindful of the promises he made, and also with unrelenting vengeance. Or, consider sacred kingship and the promise of land, biblical themes whose imaginative impact extended deeply into Western history. Hebrew kingship bred messianism, the notion of an anointed Savior figure, in its Jewish and Christian, political and mystical manifestations. In the West, the divinely sanctioned kingship was invoked by monarchic rulers far into the nineteenth and twentieth centuries as a means of legitimating political power. The biblical promise of land, coupled with the election of a people—ideas constitutive of Judaism—sanctioned the concept of the territorialization of religious faith which helped nourish Western (and non-Western) patterns of nation-building.[2] The one text perennially cited even by those who are not in the habit of invoking the Bible is Job, whose agonizing lament forces the issue of God's designs in the face of human suffering. Social conduct as antithetical as ascetic withdrawal from the world and social engagement in it found inspiration in different biblical texts. Biblical themes and stories served as justification for slavery in the United States and apartheid in South Africa, but it was likewise biblical stories and sayings that furnished moral courage and a rationale for the enhancement of civil rights and liberation from slavery. More recently, Christians have come to recognize the blood-stained nature of certain gospel verses which contributed to the incalculable

---

2. Benedict R. Anderson, *Imagined Communities: Reflections on the Origin and Spread of Nationalism*, 2nd ed. (New York: Verso, 1991).

barbarism of anti-Jewishness. But it is undeniable as well that prophetic voices and gospel proclamation have refined our sense of self-criticism and moral responsiveness. In our own present, the Bible has become at once a global market product, accessible in multimedia format, and a cultural icon, monumentalized and petrified, and yet seemingly inexhaustible as a source of spiritual and social renewal in Latin America, Africa, South Korea, in parts of the former Soviet Union, and Western countries alike.

THE TRAUMA OF HISTORY AND
THE RECTITUDE OF THE TRADITION

The picture we have drawn of the Bible's susceptibility to plural and disparate readings runs counter to modernity's sense of literalism and objectivity, and may impress us as reckless and chaotic. But it is worth remembering that the notion of the Bible as carrier of multiple senses is deeply rooted in the Christian tradition. Medieval Christianity sanctioned plural readings, not, of course, in the sense of uncontrolled randomness, but instead tamed by deep reflection on the manifold potentials inherent in sacred scripture. Couched in more linguistic terms, the Church practiced a carefully constructed hermeneutics of multiple readings. It was a deep conviction of patristic and medieval exegetes that one could not incarcerate the immense complexities of the Bible in the prisonhouse of a single sense. To the contrary, the Bible was meant to inspire readers and hearers to reach out for new meanings and to explore higher and deeper senses hidden beneath and above the literal sense.

Throughout the Middle Ages metaphors such as body and soul, letter and Spirit, were used to designate different levels of meaning and to construct multiple interpretations of biblical texts. There was, at the very least, the literal sense and the spiritual or allegorical sense, and the two stood in a hierarchical, although not necessarily oppositional, relationship. For the most part, the literal sense had no *raison d'être* on its own terms; ideally it served as a bridge toward the real goal of Bible reading: the spiritual sense, or the vision of God.

A dominant practice of medieval Bible reading was governed by the theory of the fourfold sense. Magnificently reconstructed by Henri de Lubac,[3] the theory suggested that every biblical text was amenable to four different readings: the literal sense; the allegorical sense, which gestured toward deeper meanings beyond and above the literal sense; the moral, ethical sense; and the

---

3. Henri de Lubac, *Exégèse Médiévale: Les Quatres Sens de l'Ecriture*, 4 vols. (Paris: Aubier, 1959–64).

spiritual sense, which pointed toward heavenly realities. Whether one acknowledged this fourfold sense, or merely practiced the twofold sense, or a threefold one, the spiritual sense was in all instances accorded the position of primacy.

Medieval hermeneutics was dazzling in its ability to accommodate diverse and heterogeneous biblical readings within a model of unity. There was freedom to examine the literal, grammatological specificity of individual, biblical texts; a wide latitude toward allegorical nuances and transformations of meaning; and a judicious regard for moral sensibility—provided it was understood that the spiritual exposition served as final arbiter of eternal verities. What gave unity to diversity was the premise of the Bible as the Word of God. It meant, among other things, that the Bible was perceived to be a single communication, undergirded by a unifying intentionality. In sermons and writings, medieval theologians could move through the whole Bible, citing Paul and the Psalms, Genesis and John's apocalypse, in seemingly indiscriminate fashion because they were of the conviction that the Bible embodied an indivisible message rather than a heterogeneous collection of separate books.[4]

As one moves into the high and late medieval theology one observes a tendency in some quarters to devote a greater part of biblical exegesis to the exploration of the literal sense. In the twelfth century Hugh and Andrew at the Abbey of St. Victor in Paris, for example, made the study of the literal, authorially intended sense the principal subject of their scriptural scholarship. Hugh poked fun at those who hurried over the literal sense in their eagerness to reach the mystery. Of Andrew, Beryl Smalley wrote, "No western [Christian] commentator before him had set out to give a purely literal interpretation of the Old Testament." "One sometimes rubs one's eyes," Smalley continued, observing a twelfth-century Christian theologian reading the Old Testament in an entirely nonchristological fashion and getting away with it.[5] Significantly, neither Hugh nor Andrew challenged the primacy of the spiritual sense. They justified their devotion to the literal sense as an effort to strengthen the foundation of the spiritual sense.

In the fourteenth and fifteenth centuries the philosophical school of nominalism rethought matters of mind and language in ways that served as harbinger

---

4. As far as Augustine was concerned, see, for example, Peter Brown, *Augustine of Hippo* (Berkeley: University of California Press, 1969), 254: "His memory, trained on classical texts, was phenomenally active. In one sermon, he could move through the whole Bible, from Paul to Genesis and back again, via the Psalms, piling half-verse on half-verse."

5. Beryl Smalley, *The Study of the Bible in the Middle Ages* (Oxford: Basil Blackwell, 1952), 83–195.

of a new day. William of Ockham (1285?–1349?) questioned the prevailing medieval notion that language, including biblical language, signified spiritual realities that existed outside human cognition. As a consequence of his skepticism regarding the reality of spiritual universals, he moved the contingent, the experiential, and the historical to the center of inquiry. With regard to the Bible and biblical exegesis, Ockham's nominalism paid special attention to the particular and distinctive status of texts. Scripture, indeed all texts, were assumed to be operating according to an intrinsic, linguistic economy; and operations of the mind, everybody's mind, were such that they could access textual meanings. Given these intellectual developments, nominalism subtly but discernibly enhanced the prestige of the literal sense.[6]

When in the sixteenth century Luther elevated the literal sense of the Bible, he was still moving in the tradition of the Victorines and Ockham's nominalism. But when he proceeded to denounce the fourfold sense in favor solely of the literal sense, and to condemn allegorical interpretation with particular vehemence, he was turning against a millennium and a half of Christian reading of the Bible. Scripture, he claimed, was self-explanatory. The Bible spoke for itself or, as he would phrase it, it was its own interpreter. The *sensus literalis* spoke clearly and unambiguously. Comprehensible in its plain sense and unimpeded by all other senses, the Bible was, therefore, accessible to everyone. No longer an impenetrable mystery safeguarded by and for theological experts, it was now held to be an open text intelligible for all who could hear and read.[7]

In operational practice, however, scripture was anything but a self-regulating body, and Luther did his best to promote his preferred readings by means of his own translations, interlinear and marginal glosses, scholia (brief or longer essays), introductions, illustrations, and theologically motivated arrangements of the printed text.[8] For Protestants, the Lutheran innovations marked the end of medieval mystification and signaled a welcome democratization of Bible

---

6. J. Klein, "Ockham, Wilhelm von (ca. 1285–1349)," *RGG* 4, 3rd ed. (1960): 1556–62.

7. Luther's dissociation from medieval biblical exegesis was the result of a lengthy process. See Wilhelm Pauck, *Luther: Lectures on Romans* (Philadelphia: Westminster Press, 1961), and esp. his "General Introduction," xvii–lxvi. Luther's lectures on Romans (begun at Easter 1515 and completed in September 1516) were in many ways still steeped in medieval exegetical methods. The later Luther grew fond of and was increasingly influenced by the Franciscan Nicholas of Lyra, a converted Jew, whose knowledge of Hebrew and Jewish commentaries on the Hebrew Bible caused him— among other reasons—to tone down and gradually reject the allegorical exegesis.

8. Mark U. Edwards Jr., *Printing, Propaganda, and Martin Luther* (Berkeley: University of California Press, 1994), 109–30.

reading. To Catholics, however, the novel approach to biblical hermeneutics appeared in a different light. Steeped in the tradition of medieval exegesis, they saw in the triumph of the *via moderna* a rational degradation of the mysterious quality of the Bible and a rise of the tyranny of the single sense. Whereas "at the beginning [of the Middle Ages] texts were seen as a boundless resource from which one could take an inexhaustible supply of meanings; at the end of the period, the meaning of the text is austerely anchored in the textual evidence."[9] And it was this austere single-mindedness of textual meaning that became a model for the modern, historical reading of the Bible.

In the scientific, artistic, and humanistic culture of the seventeenth, eighteenth, and nineteenth centuries the single sense came increasingly to be read in a factual representational manner. To render the texture of life and nature as closely and realistically as possible was taken to be a desirable and often unproblematic task. Among the circumstances that contributed to the elevation of the representational sense was a scientific turn toward nature propelled by a growing conviction that the natural world was readable and accessible to the observing mind. There was one way of reading the book of nature and one language that matched the observed data. In the history of art, for example, seventeenth-century Dutch painting exhibited a particular devotion to lifelike realism.[10] What motivated painters like Vermeer, Saendredam, and others was less thematic remembrance, or rhetorical persuasion, or religious veneration, or narrative explication, but rather a desire to explore the visible and concrete world minutely. Their ambition was to shun interpretation in the interest of representation. The nineteenth century was "the golden age of the novel,"[11] when the prose narrative reached a point of culmination in the realistic narrative as exemplified by such master narrators as Honoré de Balzac, Thomas Hardy, Anthony Trollope, Charlotte and Emily J. Brontë, Fedor M. Dostoevski, Leo Nikolaevitch Tolstoy, Gustave Flaubert, and others. The ideal novel was now expected to be true to life and closely based on experience, depicting society with utmost realism and devotion to detail, and delineating human nature with great depth of analytical perception. The nineteenth century also saw an unprecedented flourishing of historiography as a scientific discipline. Historians of the stature of Jules Michelet, Leopold von Ranke,

---

9. David R. Olson, *The World on Paper: The Conceptual and Cognitive Implications of Writing and Reading* (Cambridge: Cambridge University Press, 1994), 143–44.

10. Svetlana Alpers, *The Art of Describing: Dutch Art in the Seventeenth Century* (Chicago: University of Chicago Press, 1983).

11. Paul Ricoeur, *Time and Narrative*, vol. 2, trans. Kathleen McLaughlin and David Pellauer (Chicago: University Press of Chicago, 1985), 9.

Theodor Mommsen, Alexis de Tocqueville, Jakob Burckhardt, and others developed precise methods of research that taught us how to collect, categorize, and evaluate primary sources. Governed by the conviction that it was both possible and desirable to know the past as it actually happened, they produced works on aspects of European and North American history which rank among the classics of Western historiography. In these and other developments of seventeenth-, eighteenth-, and nineteenth-century scientific, artistic, and humanistic culture, the single sense and its representative content were enforced with unprecedented resolve.

The text of the Bible could not escape the scrutiny of representational thinking. We saw how the Reformers themselves had been a driving force toward the *via moderna* of the single sense. But in order to appreciate the challenge the historical method posed to Bible reading, we must remember that for Luther and Protestant orthodoxy the literal sense still encompassed a wider margin of meanings than for modern historiography. A gospel, for example, was perceived to be a story narrated by an evangelist and representing the history of its subject matter. There was a coherence between the narrative depiction and the reality it referred to. The narrative plot and the narrative's assumed historicity were still united in the literal sense which for believers was the Word of God.[12] The impact of modern representational thought was to split the literal sense into a narratological, or theological, or kerygmatic reading on one side and a literal, historical reading on the other. Luther's literal sense, already the result of a significant reduction of medieval hermeneutics, was now further reduced to the historical, factual. If the narrated, theological Jesus could no longer be assumed to be identical with the historical one, then the historical Jesus became the central focus of modernity's search for the single, representational sense. Such was the intellectual climate that invited, indeed necessitated, the search for the historical Jesus.

This modern seriousness that wanted to know what really happened engendered "a revolution in the morality of knowledge"[13] that has traumatized Christian relations with the Bible ever since. Once Holy Scripture was, methodically and without reserve, subjected to fact-finding, literal scrutiny, its desacralization as Word of God was an inescapable consequence. Perhaps no biblical text was more deeply affected by the historical method than the gospels. When, for example, the question of how the gospels had historically

---

12. Hans W. Frei, *The Eclipse of Biblical Narrative: A Study in Eighteenth and Nineteenth Century Hermeneutics* (New Haven: Yale University Press, 1974), 18–41.

13. Van Austin Harvey, *The Historian and the Believer: The Morality of Historical Knowledge and Christian Belief* (New York: Macmillan, 1966), 103.

come into existence was vigorously pursued, manufacture and human artifice were inevitably found to be involved in their compositional history. The discovery of sources, transmission and revision of materials, and the final imprint of redactional signatures gave rise to a rational concept of the gospels' genetic prehistory which left little room for divinely inspired authorial evangelists. As far as content was concerned, the drive to know, predictably enough, seized upon Jesus' miracles, his transfiguration and resurrection—stories whose character was judged to be incompatible with the canons of historical realism. Apart from examining these so-called supernatural stories, the historical method extended its critical range across the entire gospel narratives and problematized their seemingly natural, lifelike character. They did not measure up to the new seriousness that was striving after the single representational sense in hopes of finding the definitive, historical life of Jesus. Whatever else the gospels were— theological, mythological, kerygmatic stories—they were by and large not representational in the sense of reproducing the historical Jesus of the past.

In light of the rise of the single, representational sense and a growing decline of the historical credibility of the gospels, the search for the Jesus of history becomes intelligible as a project in its own right. If the gospels were written some time after and not in full conformity with the facts, what were the facts? And, if the gospels were not, or not entirely, historically representational stories, was there a way to reach behind the texts to capture the "real" Jesus of history? In view of the four gospel interpretations, was there a method to access the bedrock of the single historical origin? Questions and concerns of this kind provided an impetus for the quest of the historical Jesus. Beginning in the late seventeenth century and extending down to our own present, spanning a period of approximately three centuries, the work of the historical reconstruction of the life and death of Jesus has continued unabated. A seemingly interminable stream of lives of Jesus, written by Christians and Jews, scholars and novelists, believers and agnostics, testifies to a passionate pursuit of the single, historical truth in the Christian tradition.

This quest is fraught with deep irony because in spite of its craving for the historical origin it has in effect yielded a multitude of different versions. In the eighteenth and nineteenth centuries Jesus was variously portrayed as the greatest Utopian who combined supreme moral and spiritual ideals with a firm belief in the renewal of the world, or as the apocalyptic Son of man who was crushed by the wheels of history as he intended to transform it, or as a preacher of the interiorized presence of the Kingdom who forswore all apocalyptic fantasies, or as a political revolutionary intent on establishing an earthly Kingdom and delivering the Jews from Roman occupation, or as a Jewish reformer who brought remembrance of the great principles laid down in the

Law and the prophets. This inability to arrive at the single representation of the life of Jesus is not limited to past scholarship, when it could reasonably be argued that the historical method was still lacking in methodological exactitude. But plural versions also typify the current search in all its methodological sophistication. For Morton Smith, Jesus represents the social type of magician whose claim to be the Son of God was based on his miracles, and who attracted a following primarily through healings and exorcisms.[14] For Edward Schillebeeckx, Jesus proclaimed and instituted redemption for all Israel without exception, and made the prayer to God as abba the unconventional center of his religious experience.[15] For E. P. Sanders, Jesus was a Jewish prophet who viewed himself as eschatological agent appointed to usher in the Kingdom of God in conjunction with the destruction and rebuilding of the temple.[16] For Marcus Borg, Jesus stood in the charismatic tradition of Judaism which cultivated an intense experience of the Spirit and a conduct of holiness.[17] For Elisabeth Schüssler Fiorenza, Jesus saw himself as child of lady Wisdom, who introduced the presence of the Kingdom in the form of egalitarian communities with women in leadership positions.[18] For Burton Mack, Jesus arose from dominantly Hellenistic Galilee, practiced itinerancy, and engaged in a style of social critique that was uninvolved in specifically Jewish issues but analogous to the Hellenistic popular philosophy of Cynicism.[19] It is difficult not to agree with Luke T. Johnson's observation that the recent production of historical lives of Jesus has developed "images of Jesus that are remarkably diverse if not mutually incompatible."[20] John D. Crossan concurs: "it seems we can have as many pictures as there are exegetes" exhibiting a "stunning diversity [that] is an academic embarrassment."[21]

---

14. Morton Smith, *Jesus the Magician* (San Francisco: Harper and Row, 1878).

15. Edward Schillebeeckx, *Jesus: An Experiment in Christology*, trans. Hubert Hoskins (New York: Seabury Press, 1979).

16. E. P. Sanders, *Jesus and Judaism* (Philadelphia: Fortress Press, 1985).

17. Marcus J. Borg, *Jesus, a New Vision: Spirit, Culture, and the Life of Discipleship* (San Francisco: Harper and Row, 1987).

18. Elisabeth Schüssler Fiorenza, *In Memory of Her: A Feminist Theological Reconstruction of Christian Origins* (New York: Crossroad, 1983).

19. Burton L. Mack, *A Myth of Innocence: Mark and Christian Origins* (Philadelphia: Fortress Press, 1988).

20. Luke Timothy Johnson, *The Real Jesus: The Misguided Quest for the Historical Jesus and the Truth of the Traditional Gospels* (San Francisco: Harper/Collins, 1966), 85.

21. John Dominic Crossan, *The Historical Jesus: The Life of a Mediterranean Jewish Peasant* (San Francisco: Harper/Collins, 1991), xxviii.

How are we to explain the diversity and mutual contradictions of the multiple versions of the life of Jesus? In part, the answer lies in the data each author has moved to the center of his or her investigative probings. It makes a difference whether one highlights Jesus' deeds or discourse, his miracles or the so-called cleansing of the temple, or his ethical or apocalyptic sayings. Some authors privilege one or two gospels, others harmonize all four, while some deny all credibility to the gospel accounts and remake Jesus in the context of Greco-Roman, Jewish history. Recently, the sayings source (gospel) of Q and the extracanonical gospel of Thomas have become favorite candidates for retrieving Jesus' original message. It clearly makes a difference whether reconstructive efforts are based on the canonical gospels, on the pregospel source of Q, or on a single literary stratum of Q. Thus, the selective use of data partially explains the plurality of different versions. But selectivity also raises deeper questions about the principles and criteria underlying the use of different materials. When we observe Reimarus enacting a political and Schweitzer an apocalyptic scenario, Renan staging a pastoral setting and Schüssler Fiorenza invoking principles of gender egalitarianism, Sanders privileging a Jewish and Mack a Hellenistic milieu,[22] do we not discern here prefigurations of historical and ideological themes which in turn sway the selection and evaluation of data? Do we not perceive in the host of realistic lives of Jesus, no matter how well endowed with theoretical apparatus and historical erudition, precritical commitments to making Jesus uniquely relevant, or deliberately irrelevant, to present times? Do we not observe here the placement of current needs at the origin so as to make it communicative to the present? In any case, there is deep irony to the phenomenon of the quest that undertook to find the single, original life of Jesus and proliferated a vast plurality of different, and often mutually contradictory, works.

Modernity's representational mode of thinking and the trauma it inflicted upon traditional Christian readings of the Bible did not go unchallenged. Alarmed by the effects of the historical quest to discredit the viability of the gospel narratives, Martin Kähler, writing toward the end of the nineteenth

---

22. Hermann Samuel Reimarus, *Concerning the Intention of Jesus and His Teaching*, ed. Charles H. Talbert and trans. Ralph S. Fraser (Philadelphia: Fortress Press, 1970), 59–269 (first published in 1778 by Gotthold Ephraim Lessing as *Vom Zwecke Jesu und seiner Juenger*); Albert Schweitzer, *The Quest of the Historical Jesus*, intro. James M. Robinson (New York: Macmillan, 1968), 330–97 (first published in 1906 as *Von Reimarus zu Wrede: Eine Geschichte der Leben-Jesu-Forschung*); Ernest Renan, *The Life of Jesus* (New York: Random House, 1972), first published in 1863 as *La Vie de Jésus*; Fiorenza, *In Memory of Her*; Sanders, *Jesus and Judaism*; Mack, *Myth of Innocence*.

century, introduced an alternative approach that was to become as influential as the quest itself.[23] The "entire Life-of-Jesus movement," he argued, was based on misperceptions and bound to end in "a blind alley." There was the problem of the unreliability of historical research that failed to come up with "a solid core of the content of faith;... for the outlines and actual features of his [Jesus'] life vary continuously with the changing results of biblical research."[24] Kähler, in other words, was asking how what seemed to be accidents of historiography could be taken seriously as far as ascertaining truth and redemption was concerned. But what troubled him even more deeply than the fluctuating opinions of historians was biblical historiography itself, a project whose scientific mode of operation laid claim to foundational religious knowledge. Can the historical method legitimately access, illuminate, and demonstrate the truth of biblical texts? On this issue, Kähler professed serious doubt: reconstructions of events of the past are incapable of addressing the human condition in the present because "historical facts which first have to be established by science cannot as such become experiences of faith." Kähler's argument is of a theological kind, and it borders on the Reformation principle of justification by faith which, when applied to historical biblical research, states that faith cannot be based on the works of history lest it ceases to be pure faith. "Therefore, Christian faith and a history of Jesus repel each other like oil and water."[25] Historical facts and the experience of faith are incompatible categories.

With Kähler the distinction between the historical Jesus and the biblical Christ was institutionalized in modern theology. The historical Jesus is relegated to an indistinct figure of the past, concealed behind the gospels, and of little or no account for Christian faith. The gospels, on the other hand, are viewed as postresurrection "testimonies and confessions of believers in Christ,"[26] which carry the living Christ by way of apostolic preaching into the lives of the faithful. The resurrection, both as event and present experience of believers, is thus a key element in Kähler's understanding of the gospels and their

---

23. Martin Kähler, *The So-Called Historical Jesus and the Historic, Biblical Christ*, trans., ed. with intro. Carl E. Braaten (Philadelphia: Fortress Press, 1964); the principal essay from which the book derived its title was first published in 1892 as *Der sogenannte historische Jesus und der geschichtliche, biblische Christus*. Concerning the many works on Kähler, see esp. the study on his theology by Heinrich Leipold, *Offenbarung und Geschichte als Problem des Verstehens* (Gütersloh: Gütersloher Verlagshaus, 1962).

24. Kähler, *So-Called Historical Jesus*, 46, 103.

25. Ibid., 74.

26. Ibid., 92.

impact on hearers.[27] From this perspective, the search for the historical Jesus behind the gospels was tantamount to a misreading of the religious nomenclature of the gospels; essentially confessional texts designed to proclaim the living or risen Christ were scrutinized for their assumed documentary evidence. In addition, passages from the Old Testament were also considered to project an image of Christ which conformed to that of the New Testament. Kähler's biblical Christ, therefore, represents a uniform image or persona, present in the Old and New Testament, and functioning as redeemer of human sin and guilt.

One may plausibly contend that Kähler's model signifies a strategy of defense directed against modernity's fact-finding ethos and the threat it posed to Christian readings of the gospels. The dichotomy of the historical Jesus versus the biblical Christ appears to have been intended to carve out a zone of invulnerability around the gospels and the so-called biblical Christ, shielding them from the corrosive influence of historical curiosity, while delegitimizing the search for the historical Jesus.

Kähler's impressive alternative to the historical quest has carried significant weight in Christian theology. It dominated the so-called neo-orthodox or dialectical theology in the first half of the twentieth century and extended its influence far into our own present. As different as the theological projects of a Karl Barth, Rudolf Bultmann, and Paul Tillich were, they were all united in the conviction that the Christ proclaimed in the gospels and not the Jesus reconstructed from history was the valid object of faith.

For Barth, faith in the biblical Christ entailed the negation of all human self-assertion, including the reconstruction of the historical origins of Christian faith. Bultmann, without equal among historians of the New Testament, squarely placed Christian origins into the syncretism of the Jewish, Hellenistic, gnostic milieu of late antiquity. But he also felt the need to immunize faith from the effects of his own scholarship by contending that the biblical Christ and the proclamation about him could neither be verified nor disproven by historical science. Tillich viewed it as a distortion of the meaning of faith if it was identified with belief in the historical validity of the biblical stories.[28]

In our time, Luke Timothy Johnson's *The Real Jesus* typifies Kähler's alternative model to the historical quest.[29] Johnson entertains acutely negative views of the contemporary quest in general and of the Jesus Seminar in particular.

---

27. Ibid., 65: "The risen Lord is not the historical Jesus behind the Gospels, but the Christ of the apostolic preaching, of the whole New Testament."

28. See Braaten's introduction to Kähler's *So-Called Historical Jesus*, 32–38, and esp. 35: "With some warrant one can speak of the methodological monophysitism in Kähler and dialectical theology if this means only that the historical method cannot objectively demonstrate the revelation upon which faith stands."

The questers, he states, proceed on the assumption that history serves as a measure for theology in the sense that it can provide a theological norm for the reform of the church. That, he writes, represents typically Protestant and specifically Lutheran presuppositions. Just as Luther retrieved the original language and theological principles in the New Testament as criteria for exposing the perceived inadequacy of the medieval Church, so do the questers seek to retrieve the historical Jesus in order to uphold him vis-à-vis the perceived decline of subsequent Christian developments. History as a corrective of Christian dogma and theology—that has been the principal agenda of the quest, past and present. Johnson views the captivity of and to the historical exactitude of Jesus sayings as one of "the saddest paradoxes about the Jesus Seminar," because it thereby "shares the same literalness and historical positivism that characterizes fundamentalism"—one of the principal targets of the seminar. "The Seminar's obsessive concern with historicity and its extreme literalism merely represents the opposite side of fundamentalism." But what is it about Christianity, asks Johnson, that justifies the assumption that "the origin of a religion defines its essence"?[30]

When we ask Johnson why history, and a Jesus reconstructed from historical reality, cannot sustain faith, we receive a series of answers that in the main are reminiscent of Kähler. There is, first, the issue of historical source materials. While the archaeological, sociological, and textual advances in knowledge about the ancient Mediterranean world have been virtually unparalleled in this century, they did "not," claims Johnson, "add anything to our knowledge of his [Jesus'] life in that world." This includes the stunning discoveries at Qumran and those near Nag Hammadi which, according to Johnson, have left us for the most part with unfulfilled expectations as far as new information about the historical Jesus is concerned.[31] Second, as stated before, Johnson, along with many others, is perturbed by the remarkable plurality and diversity of contemporary historical lives of Jesus.[32] This bewildering assortment of scholarly reconstructions of Jesus' life, each claiming authenticity and originality, takes us into the realm of "fantasies and abstractions,"[33] rendering the historical quest meaningless.

---

29. The connection between Johnson and Kähler was recognized in a very perceptive review of Johnson's *The Real Jesus* by Sharon Dowd in the *Lexington Theological Quarterly* 31, no. 2 (1996): 179–83.

30. Johnson, *The Real Jesus*, 68, 26, 27, 15.

31. Johnson, "The Humanity of Jesus: What's at Stake in the Quest for the Historical Jesus" (see chap. 2).

32. Johnson, *The Real Jesus*, 85–86.

33. Johnson, "Humanity of Jesus."

But the third and most significant reason for the failure of the quest has to do less with source materials and the heterogeneity of reconstructions, and more with Jesus himself as perceived in the New Testament and in Christian faith. "Christianity in its classic form has not based itself on the ministry of Jesus but on the resurrection of Jesus, the claim that after his crucifixion and burial he entered into the powerful life of God, and shares that life... with those who can receive it." As far as the canonical gospels are concerned, they are "narratives of faith"; they are written from the standpoint of Jesus' resurrection, and they view him from the perspective of faith in the risen son of God.[34] The memory of his continuous and powerful presence is preserved and cultivated by the Church to the effect that "for the Christian confession, the risen Lord still powerfully alive is the 'real Jesus,'" and believers direct their faith not to the historical Jesus but to the living Christ. It is for this reason that the writings of the New Testament are unsuitable for the project of retrieving the inviolable identity of the origin. Indeed, a reconstruction of the historical Jesus of the past for the purpose of grounding faith "would be a form of idolatry."[35]

Last, Johnson, not unlike Kähler, develops a uniform image of the Christ figure in the New Testament. Despite his awareness of discrete representations of Christ in early Christian theology, Johnson accentuates "a profound unity of understanding concerning Jesus throughout the New Testament literature"[36] with regard to "what might be called the basic pattern of his life."[37] All four gospels, Paul, Peter, and Hebrews exhibit "the same pattern of messiahship and discipleship," and a deep consistency in the character and existence of Jesus "as one of radical obedience toward God and self-disposing service toward others."[38] Unlike the historical Jesus, Johnson's biblical Christ is accessible in the texts of the New Testament and present in the community through words of proclamation.

In sum, we find Johnson's position representative of a highly influential mode of thinking that was born out of the trauma of modernity and dates back at least as far as Martin Kähler about a century ago. It is symptomatic of this interpretive tradition to view the risen Lord as the inspiration of the gospels in the sense that they function as postresurrectional narratives. It was the memory of the risen Lord that is embraced by the Church and powerfully enacted

---

34. Johnson, *The Real Jesus*, 134, 110, 143, 151; see also Johnson, "Humanity of Jesus."

35. Johnson, *The Real Jesus*, 57, 143.

36. Ibid., 152.

37. Johnson, "The Humanity of Jesus."

38. Ibid.; Johnson, *The Real Jesus*, 158, 149.

in the lives of believers. Moreover, one delegitimizes the search for the historical Jesus on grounds of its historical and theological inadequacy, and by virtue
of the confessional nature of the gospel texts. In place of the historical Jesus,
one legitimizes a single unified image of Jesus in the New Testament, or the
Bible (Kähler), thereby enforcing an unbridgeable dichotomy between the biblical Christ and the historical Jesus—the former being valid, the latter invalid
for Christian faith.

The Christ figure developed in the Kähler-Johnson tradition undercuts all
discourse with the historical quest and, for this reason alone, merits our
scrutiny. How valid is this persona of Christ who negates our historical impuls-
es to reach for factual accuracy? The premise, for example, that Christianity "in
its classic form" focused on the resurrection and not on Jesus' ministry is ques-
tionable and, as far as Latin Christianity is concerned, historically erroneous.
A substantial part of religious devotion in Western Christianity, roughly from
the eleventh to the fifteenth century, was intently focused on Christ's passion
and death.[39] In popular piety, theological treatises, sermons, art, and plays, the
physicality of Christ as wounded persona was placed at center stage. Christ's
body and blood were the object of intense fascination and prayerful meditation. This valorization of the wounded Christ evoked diverse responses among
viewers and hearers: compassion with the tormented body, sorrowful remembrance of the woeful human condition, repentant recognition of humanity's
own sinful complicity, and spiritual transformation, or at least hope for
redemption by virtue of the cleansing power of Christ's blood. We notice in
passing, but with emphasis, that the medieval cultivation of the suffering body
of Christ was, not infrequently, accompanied by manifestations of exquisitely
malevolent anti-Jewishness. At the center of the religiosity of the later Middle
Ages lay the eucharist, the rite that transformed bread into flesh. From the
twelfth century onward the Church was privileging the eucharist as the foremost sacrament, and in the fourteenth century the rite received singular recognition by virtue of the inauguration of the feast of Corpus Christi. There was
no more hallowed experience in medieval worship than the moment of the
consecration and elevation of the host, which brought into presence Christ's

---

39. Gerard S. Sloyan, *The Crucifixion of Jesus: History, Myth, Faith* (Minneapolis:
Fortress Press, 1995); Ellen M. Ross, *The Grief of God: Images of the Suffering Jesus in
Late Medieval England* (Oxford: Oxford University Press, 1997); Miri Rubin, *Corpus
Christi: The Eucharist in Late Medieval Culture* (Cambridge: Cambridge University
Press, 1991); Sarah Beckwith, *Christ's Body: Identity, Culture and Society in Late
Medieval Writings* (New York: Routledge, 1993); James H. Marrow, *Passion
Iconography in Northern European Art of the Late Middle Ages and Early Renaissance*
(Kortrijk, Belgium: Van Ghemmert Publishing, 1970).

body and facilitated communion with it. It is possible that in focusing on Christ's body and wounds medieval piety and sacramentalism did not simply venerate Christ's humanity. The flesh of the suffering body was widely perceived to be the habitat of divine presence. Divinity enfleshed in human corporeality—that may have been the experience that lay at the heart of the eucharistic celebration of Christ's body. It was in any case

> not Jesus Christ rising from the dead that this culture found so remarkable; it was the miracle that God became embodied in order to suffer on behalf of humanity that captivated the imagination of medieval Christians. God bled and wept and suffered on the cross to draw persons to Godself; God bled and wept and suffered on the cross to manifest the boundless mercy of divine compassion.[40]

Whatever objections one may have about the quest for the historical Jesus, they cannot, therefore, be based on the assumption that Christianity "in its classic form" took no account of the physical, human Jesus in the interest of the risen Christ. To the contrary. Medieval Latin Christianity in its verbal, pictorial, and sacramental manifestations valorized the broken and wounded body of Christ, making him the center of religious life.[41]

Johnson's other argument, that the canonical gospels were written from the perspective of Jesus' resurrection, is equally problematic. It is a thesis dear to the Kähler-Johnson tradition and restated many times—despite the absence of tangible proof. Perhaps one might say that the thesis is unprovable, unarguable even. But we are today in a better position to address the issue of the generic identity and compositional nature of the canonical gospels than Kähler was about a century ago. Owing to the recent discoveries of Christian gospels near Nag Hammadi in Upper Egypt our comparative perspective on gospel literature has been substantially broadened and refined.[42]

---

40. Ross, *Grief of God*, 137.

41. In countering Johnson's claim that "Christianity in its classic form has based itself not on the ministry of Jesus but on the resurrection of Jesus" (*The Real Jesus*, 134), we have drawn attention to the Western medieval emphasis on the passion and death of Christ. Over and above the emphasis on the wounded persona of Christ, much needs to be said about the memorial (e.g., liturgical, homiletical, devotional, iconographic) cultivation of Jesus' words and deeds: Sermon on the Mount, adoration of the magi, annunciation, temptation, exorcisms, healings, feedings, transfiguration, and so on.

42. James M. Robinson, ed., *The Nag Hammadi Library in English*, 4th rev. ed. (Leiden: E. J. Brill, 1996).

Among the diverse literary genres found in the Nag Hammadi codices is a type of gospel that consists entirely of Jesus sayings and discourses. This gospel, or revelation discourse, operates largely without a narrative syntax that would connect these sayings into a single narrative plot and implant them in temporality—after the fashion of the canonical gospels. Appropriately, the Jesus who speaks these words of wisdom is not the earthly figure but rather the present, living Lord. In texts such as the *Apocryphon of James*, the *Apocryphon of John*, the *Gospel of Thomas*, the *Book of Thomas the Contender* (in part), the *Gospel of Mary* (in part), the *Dialogue of the Savior*, the *Sophia of Jesus Christ*, the first and second *Apocalypse of James*, the *Acts of Peter and the Twelve* (in part), and the *Letter of Peter to Philip* it is the luminous Christ who addresses a select group of male and female disciples, or one of his brothers. It is in these documents, which are absent from the canon, that we encounter the genre of a sayings or discourse gospel in which the living Christ—in the absence of any narration of his earthly existence—constitutes the starting point of his revelatory words of wisdom. Here we encounter a gospel genre that is constructed from the point of view of what in the orthodox tradition would be called Easter. This is what the gospel looks like which Kähler, Johnson, and many others have in mind when they invoke the risen or living Christ authoritatively positioned for the purpose of delivering postresurrectional testimonies and confessions. But this Kähler-Johnson model is ideally exemplified by the extracanonical gospel of Thomas, and not the canonical gospel of Mark, the latter focusing on the earthly life of Jesus culminating in his crucifixion and in the end withholding the risen Christ from the disciples. Whatever objections one might have about the quest for the historical Jesus, they cannot, therefore, be based on the assumption that the canonical gospels were written from the perspective of the resurrection, and that they are for this reason in conflict with the ethos of historical curiosity.[43]

---

43. The whole issue of "gospel-resurrection" merits a more nuanced treatment than it has received in the Kähler-Johnson scholarly tradition. At least three aspects need to be differentiated. (1) Synchronically, the canonical gospel narratives culminate in death/resurrection/ascension—although with considerable thematic variations. At the same time, the gospels' narrative plots enact a host of other religious and ethical themes, configure aspects of time and space, develop characterization, and construe multiple plots and subplots. In view of these narrative complexities it is as inadmissible to call the gospels "passion narratives with an extended introduction" as it is to call them "resurrection narratives with an extended introduction." (2) Diachronically, the gospels are deeply implicated in tradition, and respond to, transform, and reabsorb traditional elements of various kinds. In view of the gospels' plural compositional engagements it is inadmissible to claim that they were written singly from the perspective of

How valid, finally, is this single, unified persona called the biblical Christ that Johnson extricates from the texts of the New Testament? His model of the biblical Christ calls for thoughtful probing since it claims the authority to replace, indeed delegitimize, the Jesus of history. Our reflections will be limited to the Jesus figure(s) exhibited in the four canonical gospels. Beginning in the 1960s a growing number of biblical scholars began to focus on the biblical Christ by paying (renewed) attention to the gospel narratives. Responding to the trauma of modernity—which had split the Jesus of history from the biblical Christ—one refocused from events behind the gospels to the world inside the gospels. But instead of aspiring to a single persona underlying all four gospels, one took seriously the discrete literary map and singular representation of each individual gospel. Since the gospels were losing credibility before the ever-more-vigilant tribunal of modern historiography, they were now reexamined in light of what they appeared to be, namely four separate narratives. Johnson not only welcomed this move toward a narrative appreciation of the gospels, but at an early stage contributed substantially to a literary reading of Luke-Acts.[44] Instead of viewing the gospels as obstacles that needed to be overcome in order to get to what really mattered, namely history, one now paid attention to the gospels' own narrative world. When thus read narratively, the gospels displayed compositional properties that were deep-rooted in literary discourse: arrangements of individual stories and dialogues; threefold repetitions and dualities; the splicing of one story into halves for the purpose of framing another story; narrative uptakes of antecedent themes; the circumspect use of christological titles; flashbacks that link up with characters and themes in the Hebrew Bible, and prolepses whose realization lies outside the narrative world; plot constructions frequently accomplished by the dynamics of conflict; narrative insights into the innermost feelings of characters, dialogues, for example, between Jesus and the disciples, accessible to both the disciples and the readers of the gospels, vis-à-vis narrative asides exclusively accessible to the readers, who always know more than the characters in the

---

Jesus' resurrection. (3) In oral performance or in reading (aloud or even in silence) a participatory element enters into the hermeneutical process. But the oral/readerly experience is by no means in all instances synonymous with that of the risen Lord. A miracle story, for example, invites hearers/readers to respond to, or participate in, or empathize with the narrated events, and to reorient their lives accordingly. A parabolic performance may not carry any christological features vis-à-vis hearers/readers. In view of these performative dynamics, it is inadmissible to claim that the memory of the Church always activates the presence of the risen Lord.

44. Luke Timothy Johnson, *The Literary Function of Possessions in Luke-Acts,* SBL Dissertation Series 39 (Missoula, Mont.: Scholars Press, 1977).

gospels. In short, we have learned to read the gospels with what Ricoeur has called a "second naiveté,"[45] no longer with a critical view toward its assumed historicity, but rather with an appreciative eye for its narrative world.

This new focus on the literary character of the gospels has sensitized us to the different modes of construction that have gone into the making of each gospel. Such are the differences that they amount to four rather distinct narrative configurations of the life, death, and resurrection of Jesus. But once a separate narrative integrity is conceded to each gospel, it is no longer possible to read one gospel through the spectacles of another, or to unite all four together in a single composite model. Each narrative configuration deserves to be apprehended on its own terms and in its own right. As far as christology is concerned, each narrative representation of Jesus in Mark, Matthew, Luke, and John merits separate attentiveness as far as their thematic developments and interlacing with their respective plot structures are concerned. As narrative criticism, therefore, has come to view this matter, we are confronted with a plurality of gospel christologies that are reducible to a single christological proposition only at the steep price of violating their separate narrative integrity. This new awareness of the plurality of gospel constructions problematizes Johnson's projection of a single unified image of Jesus in the New Testament. His is the construction of a biblical Christ who in this monolithic singularity evades, indeed negates, one of the more noteworthy features of New Testament christology, namely that of the plural representations of Christ. Whatever objections one might have about the quest for the historical Jesus, they cannot, therefore, be based on a single unified character of Jesus assumed to be grounded in the New Testament. In sum, Johnson's repudiation of the historical quest does not hold up under critical scrutiny.

THE RECTITUDE OF HISTORY AND
THE TRAUMA OF THE TRADITION

If in the Kähler-Johnson tradition one seizes upon the biblical Christ, exhibiting him as a single, unified persona, in the quest represented by Crossan one reclaims the Jesus of history, making him the irrefutably authoritative norm for subsequent tradition and for Christian faith alike. Both Johnson and Crossan

---

45. Paul Ricoeur, *The Symbolism of Evil*, trans. Emerson Buchanan (Boston: Beacon Press, 1967), 352. Although Ricoeur applied the concept of "second naiveté" to symbol, it is likewise applicable to narrative in the sense that postcritical sensibilities "can believe only by interpreting."

are acutely aware of the distinctive narrative emplotment of each of the four canonical gospels. But Johnson, while conceding that the gospels "are divergent in their accounts,"[46] insists that—notwithstanding their differences—they converge in fundamental patterns of christological identity. For Crossan the different narrative configurations of the gospels leave us with little choice but to retrieve the Jesus of history. If for Johnson Christian faith "has never… been based on historical reconstructions of Jesus," "but on the resurrection of Jesus,"[47] for Crossan "there is, ever and always, only one Jesus," namely the historical Jesus who in the status of the resurrection carries the wounds that "came not from heaven but from history."[48] These are the two positions, fundamentally dissimilar and essentially irreconcilable, that have asserted themselves in response to the traumatic challenge posed by modernity's ethos of historical exactitude and the demands for factual verification.

Since in Johnson's view the reconstruction of the historical Jesus for the purpose of grounding faith is theologically illegitimate, we need to inquire into the rationale, theological or otherwise, that Crossan adduces for having undertaken his monumental project of *The Historical Jesus*.[49] Why this exceptional scholarly investment in efforts to recover Jesus who in his historical singularity remains unavailable to us in any single text or source?

In his contribution to this volume Crossan lays out a theological field of vision that situates and explicates his research on the historical Jesus. He distinguishes two types of Christianity, one being of a sarcophilic and/or incarnational persuasion, and the other of a sarcophobic and/or docetic one. Derived from the Greek roots for "flesh" (*sarx*), "love" (*philia*), and "fear" (*phobos*), the sarcophilic type implies a monistic anthropology of the union of flesh and spirit, while the sarcophobic type postulates a dichotomy of flesh versus spirit. The monistic type of Christianity postulates a spirit-embodied humanity, which defies the disjunction of body from spirit, refrains from an anthropologically based gender privileging, and honors humans in their body-spirit integrity. The dualistic or docetic type Crossan declares to be thoroughly dehumanizing in its aspirations to separate the spirit from matter, to exalt spirit over matter, to equate male with spirit and female with matter, and to degrade sexuality and our humanity in that process. Christologically, sarcophilic Christianity proclaims the flesh-and-body of the earthly Jesus who as risen Lord carries the wounds of his historical execution. There is only one Jesus, the

46. Johnson, *The Real Jesus*, 108.
47. Ibid., 133, 134.
48. Crossan, "Historical Jesus as Risen Lord" (see chap. 1).
49. Ibid.

one who was incarnated in the flesh and stands in physical, material continuity with his existence as the risen One. Sarcophobic Christianity, to the contrary, holds that the earthly Jesus was only apparently real, that there is at best a spiritual continuity linking the earthly with the risen Lord, and that the spiritual, apparitional Christ, as distinct from the earthly, historical Jesus, is endowed with reality. Crossan sides with the sarcophilic type of Christianity, which in its humanizing affirmation of a nondualistic humanity and christology furnishes the theological rationale and justification for modernity's aspirations to recover the Jesus of history.

Crossan draws a sharp battle line across the spectrum of Christian traditions in ways that are surprising and astoundingly judgmental in an age of inclusiveness, ecumenism, and globalization. Perhaps more important, the thesis ill comports with the picture of Christian origins which has been emerging roughly over the last hundred years. Let us begin with three propositions that have reached the status of virtual commonplaces in the study of early Christianity, but need to be restated here in view of Crossan's thesis. First, scholarship has intentionally crossed canonical boundary lines for the purpose of accessing, capturing, and integrating the plurality of Christian voices into a more genuinely panoramic and historically representative view of Christian origins. We have developed a voracious appetite for any and all remains of the Christian past. To this end we seize upon every scrap of textual, archaeological, and pictorial evidence that becomes available to us. We seek to balance, for example, the exclusive emphasis on Latin Christianity—suggested to us by Luke-Acts and its model of Christianity's movement from Jerusalem to Rome—with a renewed focus on Syrian and Egyptian Christianity. The work in progress on ascetic and monastic movements serves to correct a tendency to think that Christianity by and large settled down in Greco-Roman household structures—a picture suggested to us by a selective reading of the canonical Pastorals. Last, but not least, we seek to recover the voices of those who were marginalized, first and foremost women, but also slaves, and Christians who practiced a homoerotic lifestyle. In its most general sense, the result has been an ever-growing awareness of the copiously diversified nature of early Christian traditions. Countless Christian prophets and teachers proclaimed similar as well as dissimilar and often contradictory messages, practiced a variety of personal and communal lifestyles, each insisting on the truthfulness of his or her version of the gospel. Such is the multiformity of Christian practice and experience that it problematizes all single-line approaches or methods.

Second, the picture we are developing of Christian origins is one not merely of diversity of viewpoints and modes of living, but of contentiousness and polemics as well. From the start, it seems, the legacy of Jesus was fiercely contested by those who pledged allegiance to him. In certain instances intra-Christian polemics were no less intense, and no less vicious, than the unfolding Christian-Jewish disputes. These intra-Christian struggles intensified in the second and third centuries, when Christian theologians began to introduce heresiological rhetoric into the debates over vital issues such as the value of martyrdom; apostolic tradition; the nature, passion, and resurrection of Jesus; ecclesiastical authority; the theological soundness of personal, visionary experiences; and so forth. By shaping the discourse in sharply divisive categories, theologians of the stature of Irenaeus, Ignatius, Hippolytus, Tertullian, and others succeeded in solidifying their own positions in confrontation with those Christians who were now labeled heretics. Christianity came to be divided into orthodoxy versus heresy.

Third, while emergent orthodoxy shaped its position vis-à-vis a plurality of alternative options, one of its major targets in the second and third centuries was a type of Christianity that came to be known as *Gnosis*.[50] Among a vast array of issues that were raised to refine and energize the identity of orthodoxy in distinction from the so-called gnostic heresy was that of the life, death, and resurrection of Jesus and his role in the Christian vision of redemption. Orthodoxy insisted on the inalienable import of Jesus' incarnation and the redemptive significance of his death, as expounded in the canonical gospels. Additionally, and most important, orthodoxy opted for a literal interpretation of Jesus' resurrection. Jesus was raised in the flesh, and anyone who denied this fact was declared heretical and denied the designation Christian. To so-called gnostic Christians it was less the earthly Jesus and his death that were deemed to be significant, but more the spiritual, living Christ. His resurrection was, therefore, understood in a spiritual, not literal, sense, and what truly mattered was the experiential and interior accessibility of and to the living Christ. This was (in part) the kind of christology that orthodoxy judged to be heretical and unworthy of the designation Christian. I take these three propositions to be broadly affirmed in contemporary studies of Christian origins, and I doubt Crossan has a major disagreement with them.

Based on this widely though not uniformly accepted synopsis of the scholarly status of Christian origins, Crossan's distinction of sarcophilic versus sarcophobic, and a monistic versus a dualistic mode of being Christian

---

50. Elaine Pagels, *The Gnostic Gospels* (New York: Penguin Books, 1982); first published in 1979 by Random House. See also Pagels's "The Orthodox against the Gnostics: Confrontation and Interiority in Early Christianity," in *The Other Side of God: A Polarity in World Religions*, ed. Peter L. Berger (Garden City, N.Y.: Anchor Press/Doubleday, 1981), 61–73.

constitutes a continuation or, if you will, revival of ancient heresiological polemics—with one major exception. Crossan recognizes that the traditional implementation of these heresiological categories is no longer workable in the sense of dividing Christianity into Catholic orthodoxy versus gnostic heresy because, as he correctly states, orthodoxy and so-called heresy each contain elements of both a monistic and a dualistic type. Catholic and gnostic Christianity are "hardly coincident with the monism and dualism under discussion."[51] This is a significant concession which has the effect of undercutting traditional lines of demarcation. But instead of abandoning the ancient heresiological nomenclature altogether, Crossan proceeds to reapply it to all Christian and, in fact, Western traditions, drawing a new line of division that redefines what constitutes orthodoxy and heresy. He sees "a profound fault-line in Western sensibility and consciousness"[52] which, simply put, divides those who believe in the separation of spirit or soul from body and those who believe in the inseparable unity of both.

We raise four questions in response to Crossan's thesis. First, if the old nomenclature of a monistic versus a dualistic type of Christianity is admittedly inapplicable for the purpose for which it was initially designed, namely to identify and separate a Catholic from a gnostic Christianity, why hold on to it in the interest of reclassifying the plurality of Christian identities into a framework that has proven inoperable? Given the vast diversity of Christian styles of spirituality and modes of personal experience, should we not tread lightly and resist the temptation of straying into the errancies of the past? Crossan's thesis is not without irony because it decries the anthropological binary divide of soul versus body only to reinvoke a historical binary divide between a sarcophobic versus a sarcophilic typology. Why reimagine Christianity in the traditional metaphors of truth versus falsehood? More finely tuned responses to the concreteness of multiple distinctions are required.

Second, can the admittedly fateful dichotomy of body versus soul or spirit summarily be invoked as an explanatory device to account for the major flaws in Western civilization? Let us take gender inequality as one of the examples cited by Crossan. How much historical weight carries his thesis that sarcophobic Christianity's repugnance toward the body was principally responsible for patriarchal oppressive features? The impression that is thereby conveyed that sarcophilic Christianity was immune to harmful gender ideology surely is open to question. Early in Christian history, for example, it was Luke who made attestation to the bodily resurrection of Jesus a qualifying criterion for apostolicity

---

51. Crossan, "Historical Jesus as Risen Lord."
52. Ibid.

(Acts 1:21–22; 10:39–41; 13:30–31). This application of "the doctrine of bodily resurrection also serves an essentially political function,"[53] because it was setting into motion a chain of command for all future generations of Christians which effectively excluded women from leadership positions. Indeed, it has been a persuasive argument in feminist studies that the development of male leadership roles, the drawing of gender boundaries, and rites of entry and exclusion were primarily social constructions.[54] Jewish, Greco-Roman, and Christian women in antiquity were burdened with structures of power that were virtually united in devising strategies of resistance to their accession to positions of equality, let alone authority. Jewish patriarchal values, Greco-Roman networks of patronage, and Christian apostolicity were all operative in support of gender inequality. It is an all-pervasive flaw in our ancient heritage, cutting across distinctions of monistic versus dualistic anthropology, and deeply rooted in institutional and political structures of power.

Third, we can no longer be certain that dualism is in all instances the most plausible explanation for the sarcophobic mortification of the flesh that exemplifies ascetic and monastic modes of Christian religiosity. Here we need to acknowledge that so-called commonsense assumptions about asceticism—its roots, objectives, and actual practices—have for some time been subjected to some rather large revisions. Two recent masterpieces written on Christian asceticism, Peter Brown's *The Body and Society*[55] and Caroline Walker Bynum's *Holy Feast and Holy Fast*,[56] are critically relevant to Crossan's configuration of Christianity. Brown chronicles the history of the repudiation of the flesh and the renunciation of sexuality in the Western and Eastern Church of the first five centuries. There can be no doubt about the intensity of suspicion many early Christians felt toward the body, about the extent to which sexual renunciation came to stand for Christian commitment, and how different Christianity was from what now goes by that name. To grasp the phenome-

---

53. Pagels, *Gnostic Gospels*, 3; see esp. chapter 1, "The Controversy over Christ's Resurrection: Historical Event or Symbol?" 3–32.

54. On the philosophical implications of feminist perspectives, see Nancy Tuana and Rosemarie Tong, eds., *Feminism and Philosophy: Essential Readings in Theory, Reinterpretation, and Application* (Boulder, Colo.: Westview Press, 1995). On feminist implications for biblical scholarship, see Adela Yarbro Collins, ed., *Feminist Perspectives on Biblical Scholarship* (Chico, Calif.: Scholars Press, 1985).

55. Peter Brown, *The Body and Society: Men, Women, and Sexual Renunciation in Early Christianity* (New York: Columbia University Press, 1988).

56. Caroline Walker Bynum, *Holy Feast and Holy Fast: The Religious Significance of Food to Medieval Women* (Berkeley: University of California Press, 1987).

non, Brown suggests, we are compelled to deal with a conglomerate of notions associated with virginity, chastity, spirituality, and a concomitant anxiety about the body—phenomena that are entrenched in diverse historical and anthropological constellations. The celebrated virgin-martyr Thecla, for example, exemplifies the social complexities surrounding her adamant refusal to marry her fiancé, a young man with a bright future in the political establishment at Iconium.[57] Her defiance of marriage was perceived—by herself, her fiancé, and the city fathers—as an attack on "family values," and it surely posed a threat to the two most treasured institutions of the Hellenistic world, the city (*polis*) and the household (*oikia*). Thecla became a role model for women not because she redeemed her spiritual self entrapped in the body but rather because she shielded her bodily autonomy from the pressures of a menacing political establishment that coerced women into the role of bearers of children. Other Christians linked their ascetic practices with particular readings of Adam and Eve's fall, viewing it as the event that had sentenced humans to a fateful cycle of sexuality and mortality. Only sexual continence, it was believed, could undo the effects of the fall and restore the original state of authenticity and freedom of will.[58] Tertullian (160?–220?), who pronounced severe judgments on instinctual stirrings and sexual fantasies, was nonetheless "not a 'dualist' in any way." It was precisely because he believed in a virtually corporeal form of the soul that mortification of the flesh could significantly impact the status of soul. In the understanding of Origen (185?–254?) the Platonist, gratification of physical sensations had the effect of dulling our genuine capacity for the spiritual pleasure of tasting, smelling, and drinking the Wisdom of God. If the Christian objective was to cultivate unremitting sexual discipline and continent bodies, the aim was not to disqualify pleasure per se, but rather to attain acutely felt, sensuous delights of a kind far superior to those the body could ever generate. The Christian monks of fourth-century Egypt became towering figures of a new humanity by living and surviving in an uninhabitable environment, standing "as a perpetual challenge to the situation of hunger and bitter dependence on the marketplace that characterized the society of a starving and laborious Near East." Gregory of Nyssa (335?–394), another Platonist, felt that what was at stake in chastity was not the repression of sexual drives, but temporality and the fear of death. Marriage for purposes of procreation was the

---

57. Brown, *Body and Society*, 156–59; Dennis Ronald MacDonald, *The Legend and the Apostle: The Battle for Paul in Story and Canon* (Philadelphia: Westminster Press, 1983).

58. Brown, *Body and Society*, 92–96. See esp. Elaine Pagels, *Adam, Eve, and the Serpent* (New York: Random House, 1988).

most obvious instrument to obstruct the sight of the grave and to repress the terror of personal extinction. Chastity, he felt, was the appropriate, the only way to overcome the pathetic urge to increase and multiply, an urge that would shorten the inexorable tick of time. "To abandon marriage was to face down death. It was to deliver no further hostages to death in the form of children."[59] These examples must suffice to convey the point Brown makes, and makes quite persuasively. Early Christian asceticism cannot be explained by or reduced to a single anthropological pattern; it is adequately understood only as a dynamic interaction of various and changing motivations, social circumstances, and anthropological convictions. Because both discourse and practices of renunciation are generally foreign to the contemporary Western experience, understanding the phenomenon makes serious demands on our imagination and "should challenge all interpreters of religion to rethink methods and approaches and questions."[60] Bynum's work, concerning the most extravagant practices of fasting and self-inflicted punishment among medieval women, forcefully repudiates the interpretation historians of religion have traditionally given to this phenomenon, namely that it was self-evidently dualistic and hence pathological. Although male theologians not infrequently interpreted women's ascetic piety as internalized dualism or misogyny, they did not, Bynum suggests, as a rule speak for the women themselves and their bodily experiences. Built on the realization that the humanity of Christ was a central religious experience for medieval women, Bynam explains their fasting and hunger, chastity and abstinence, as well as their cultivation of bodily pain as a way of "luxuriating in Christ's physicality." They strove not to eradicate their bodies, but rather to consummate extreme but latent opportunities of their flesh in order to merge their painfully sensitized bodies with the flesh of Christ whose agony was perceived to be of redemptive significance. Medieval asceticism should, therefore, "not be understood as rooted in dualism, in a radical sense of spirit opposed to or entrapped by body," but as *imitatio Christi* in the sense of "incorporation of flesh into flesh."[61] Anthropological dualism does not serve as the most adequate category of analysis for the medieval sarcophobic mortification of the flesh practiced by medieval Christian women.

Fourth, one may at least raise the question whether sarcophobic Christianity, to the extent that it was rooted in a genuine dualism of body versus soul or

---

59. Brown, *Body and Society*, 76–78, 160–77, 221, 292–304.

60. Vincent L. Wimbush, "Rhetorics of Restraint: Discursive Strategies, Ascetic Piety and the Interpretation of Religious Literature," *Semeia* 57 (1992): 3–4. On current reconceptualizations of Jewish, Greco-Roman, and Christian asceticism in antiquity and late antiquity, see *Semeia* 57 and 58 (1992).

61. Bynum, *Holy Feast and Holy Fast*, 246, 294, 257.

spirit, was in all instances as dehumanizing an experience as Crossan describes it. Could we not imagine that the idea of an inviolable interior self embedded in the perishable body gave believers a powerful sense of selfhood, dignity, and worth? What was degrading about the saying attributed to Jesus: "What does it profit a man, to gain the whole world and lose his soul?" (Mark 8:36). "Humble people everywhere, who made up the vast majority of people in antiquity, heard his [Jesus'] message and found themselves valued members of a new kind of kingdom in which quality of soul, not social position, was the measure of greatness."[62]

We have gone to what may seem inordinate lengths to diagnose the implications of a typology of being Christian in terms of a sarcophobic versus a sarcophilic tradition because it serves Crossan to situate and explicate the quest for the historical Jesus. The quest, for Crossan, is legitimated and required by the nondualistic focus on the incarnate Jesus and his bodily continuity into the status of resurrection. But what if these categories are inadequately grounded in the historical experience, hence liable to distorting the plenitude and variability of Christian traditions, and ethically flawed because they cast aspersion on a culturally and theologically significant segment of Christianity? To be sure, Crossan's theological justification, problematic as it is, does not invalidate his work as historical quester. But the reasons he advances for his work cause one to wonder why his *re*construction of the historical Jesus is associated with a serious *mis*judgment of the tradition. Earlier we saw how Johnson's negation of the quest implied a signal lack of understanding about essential aspects of medieval Christianity. Why is it that both the negator and the defender of the quest land us in such lamentable judgments about the larger landscape of the Christian tradition? This is a question to which we shall return at the conclusion of this chapter.

Crossan's rationale for the historical quest—quite apart from reviving an ancient heresiological divide—is but a subtype of a widely held view. Canonical Christianity, it is asserted, cultivated incarnational sensitivities by grounding the representation of Jesus in the flesh of humanity. It would seem inescapably obvious that the gospels are making just this point. As far as medieval Latin Christianity was concerned, we observed that it was in no small measure indebted and committed to the physicality of Jesus' body. When therefore measured by these ancient and medieval standards, modernity's reconstructive efforts vis-à-vis the historical Jesus appear to be nothing less and nothing more than a valid extension of certified christological emphases and sympathies. This is the classic incarnational argument on behalf of modernity's

---

62. Riley, *One Jesus, Many Christs*, 30.

historical quest. Plausible as it may seem, the argument nonetheless has the effect of minimizing appreciation for the gap that separates modern from medieval and ancient christological engagements. It fails to take adequate account of what we have termed the trauma of modernity which manifests itself in historical sensibility and in a passionate pursuit of the single, representational sense.

To assert that the historical figure of Jesus—represented at best indirectly in the gospels and existing at most behind the gospels—constitutes the foundational and singularly valid sense is a notion that is incompatible with most segments of ancient, patristic, and medieval Christianity.[63] At most points prior to the sixteenth century there is disinterest in or resistance to calcification of the gospel narratives into a single-minded product. But, we press further, is it not inescapably obvious that the canonical gospels in their emphasis on the earthly Jesus furnish the rationale for the modern quest of the historical Jesus? What may seem obvious to some of us was not obvious to believers for the longest period of Christian history, which has understood the gospels either rhetorically as discourse or performance inviting participation and effectuating redemption for the believer, and/or as reservoirs carrying virtually inexhaustible treasures of signification. We might also in earnest consider the implications of the canonizers' privileging of four gospels and not one. Does not the fourfold representation once again point to plural sensitivities more than to the reductionist impulse toward singularity? To be sure, cross-readings among the gospels, for example, the supplementing of one gospel with elements from another, was common practice and entirely acceptable because the Bible was perceived to be the work of a unified intentionality. To be sure, harmonizations of the four into one, such as Tatian's *Diatessaron* in the second century C.E., reflect the desire to have unity at the expense of diversity. But even gospel harmonies were designed not to reach for facts behind the text, but rather to conflate existing texts. And then there are the gospel commentaries. It is worth remembering that Christians from an early point on wrote commentaries on individual gospels, thus acknowledging the separate and discrete character of each gospel. The acceptance of four lives of Jesus strained ancient, patristic, and medieval Christianity toward the plural representations long before it took the fateful step toward historical singularity.

---

63. Not even the theological school of Antioch, which is traditionally associated with the "literal" sense, was pursuing anything remotely like the Jesus behind the gospels. Theodore of Mopsuestia and John of Chrysostom stressed the particular linguistic contextuality, and not a hypothetically reconstructed sense separate and distanced from the sacred texts.

The legitimacy of the quest can thus not simply, if at all, be derived from so-called incarnational Christianity. The intellectual roots of the quest are anything but monocausal. We mentioned the philosophical school of nominalism and its refocusing of intellectual attentiveness from the universals to the particular. It was a contributing factor to the fall of plural senses and the rise of the single sense. Nor can we overlook the invention of the movable letter type, which lay at the heart of the print medium. Typography imposed a relentless regimentation upon language, with words tidily, indeed sternly, arranged in line, with equidistant spaces between letters and words and lines respectively, with margins severely justified, producing duplicates of unprecedented sameness, and masterpieces of hitherto inexperienced aesthetic proportionality. Luther's repudiation of allegory, his insistence on the literal sense, and his argument that scripture was its own interpreter are all features unthinkable without the novel experience of the print medium and the illusion it created that language was, as it were, standing on its own. These and other cultural phenomena converged in modernity, which was and continues to be the agent of an irrepressible desire, an addiction even, to get to the facts. More than anything it is this ethos of modernity, its thirsting after knowledge as representation, its desire to recapture the evidence of regularities, the patterns of pathology, and the nexus of concrete events—to want to know, in other words, what Edith Wyschogrod has termed "the rectitude of fact"[64]—that lies at the root of the historical quest. The voracious appetite for the singular facts of Jesus' life and death is thus a child more of modernity's *curiositas*, the unquenchable thirst for factual rectitude, than of intrinsically Christian developments or necessities.[65] It is a concession to the pressures of the modern factual perspective more than the result of innate connections with a so-called incarnational, sarcophilic christology. And the price one pays for submission to the force of fact is the rational reduction of ancient, patristic, and medieval polyphonic sensibilities to the austerity of the single sense.

Modernity's quest for facticity cannot be discounted in any area of life, including the origins of Christianity. There is a sense in which we can no longer afford to lament Enlightenment's rational blueprint, its suppression of vital components of the sensorium, its apotheosis of the single sense, its inability to

---

64. Edith Wyschogrod, *An Ethics of Remembering: History, Heterology, and the Nameless Others* (Chicago: University of Chicago, 1998), 63.

65. For a masterful philosophical treatment of *curiositas* (*Neugierde*) as a symptom of modernity, see Hans Blumenberg, *The Legitimacy of the Modern Age*, trans. Robert M. Wallace (Cambridge, Mass.: MIT Press, 1983); original German: *Die Legitimitaet der Neuzeit* 2nd rev. ed. (Frankfurt/Main: Suhrkamp, 1988).

discern the fault lines within reason itself, its inclination to take truth and facts for interchangeable terms, and its belief in uninterpreted information and in data just lying there to be downloaded and called up on the screen. As truly lamentable as all these issues are, they can no longer discredit our efforts to get at the facts. At the end of this century we look back upon a history that is still bleeding profusely, an experience that renders the quest for factual truth ethically mandatory. The trauma of history in our time is not that facts disprove faith or unmask our fictions, but rather that facts themselves have become unbelievable, unthinkable, unrepresentable, and yet in dire need of rememorization. The cataclysmic genocides of this century "whose sheer magnitude and unfigurable ethical force... resists emergence in word and image"[66] nonetheless compel us to confront the facts as best as we can to rescue them from fading into oblivion and to deny the deniers of facts the last word. Facts, at the end of this century, have taken on an ethical force, and remembering factuality has become a moral imperative.

In the theological tradition reaching from Kähler to Johnson one repudiates the quest for the historical Jesus on the premise that history cannot serve as measure for theology, and that a Jesus reconstructed from history is incapable of sustaining faith. This repudiation of the quest is driven by the polarity of fact versus faith and animated by the passion to salvage faith. For Crossan the quest was validated by appeal to so-called sarcophilic Christianity at the exclusion of so-called sarcophobic Christianity. By contrast we suggest a validation of the quest as an "ethics of remembering" based on the moral force of factuality and driven by the gaping wounds of history. We privilege Jesus' facts more than our faith, for what matters in the ethics of remembering is exercising responsibility toward him, rather than guarding us and our faith.

One of the most impressive features about Crossan's reconstruction of Jesus' life is its methodological design. Few if any lives of Jesus have ever been constructed on so logical and reasonable a methodological basis and executed with such skillful consistency. No one before Crossan has deployed so judicious an apparatus of formal principles in collecting, evaluating, and classifying available Jesus materials as far as sayings and, to some extent, stories are concerned. His taxonomic and methodological competence sets imposing standards for Jesus research.[67]

The modern historian, intent on writing a life of Jesus, is confronted with Jesus materials that are embedded in various contexts of the tradition. In view

---

66. Wyschogrod, *Ethics of Remembering*, 66.

67. For the following review of Crossan's methodology, see also my article "Jesus and Tradition: Words in Time, Words in Space," *Semeia* 65 (1994): 139–67.

of this situation, Crossan calls upon historical scholarship to "search back through those sedimented layers to find what Jesus actually said and did."[68] In order to accomplish this objective, he classified the Jesus materials in terms of single, double, triple, and multiple attestation. Next he compiled a comprehensive inventory of Christian literary documents both inside and outside the canon. Based on chronological priority, he divided the early tradition into four strata, which are dated from 30 to 60, from 60 to 80, from 80 to 120, and from 120 to 150 C.E. Finally, he constructed a database that assigned single, double, triple, and multiple attested materials to their respective strata in the tradition. For reasons of space, Crossan's evaluation relied almost entirely on the first stratum, and in the interest of maximal objectivity he disregarded single attestation even in the first stratum. Hence, plurality of independent attestation and chronological priority of strata determine historical reliability of data. "A first-stratum complex having, say, sevenfold independent attestation must be given very, very serious consideration."[69]

In principle, Crossan's methodological apparatus is not designed to retrieve the original saying of Jesus. Instead, he is looking for the common denominator that underlies all plural versions of a given saying. By pruning all existent versions of a saying of its contextual and compositional variables he seeks to arrive at the essential structural stability that he has termed "the aphoristic core," or "the *ipsissima structura*,"[70] or "the core of the complex," or "a common structural plot."[71] For example, the fourfold independent attestation of the saying on "Kingdom and Children" entails an underlying "central and shocking" metaphor that goes back to Jesus. Once Crossan has decontextualized this core complex of "Kingdom and Children" from its various engagements in tradition, he recontextualizes it in a broadly designed cross-cultural matrix and in the narrower context of Hellenistic and Jewish history. When thus resituated and resuscitated, children are not a metaphor of the humble (Mark), not of those newly baptized in water and Spirit (John), and not of the presexual or nonsexual celibates (Thomas)—all variable interpretations of the tradition— but quite realistically those who have no rights, that is, nobodies. This is what one would immediately have thought of children in first-century C.E. Galilee, and this is why the core complex of "Kingdom and Children," when replanted into authentic historicity, is so shocking an idea.[72] One may wonder

---

68. Crossan, *The Historical Jesus*, xxxi.
69. Ibid., xxxii.
70. John Dominic Crossan, *In Fragments: The Aphorisms of Jesus* (San Francisco: Harper and Row, 1983), 37–66.
71. Crossan, *The Historical Jesus*, xxxiii, 261.
72. Ibid., 266–69.

whether "nobody" was the first thing that came to mind in Jewish culture of late antiquity when people saw or spoke of children. But our concern is with method, and the saying on "Kingdom and Children" exemplifies a crucial component of Crossan's methodology: comparative attention to plural and variable attestations of a saying exposes its essential core whose specific meaning is subsequently determined by reentering this core abstraction into the concrete nexus of historical causality.

"Method, method, and once again, method,"[73] Crossan exclaims, invoking something akin to an apotheosis of methodology. Indeed, his mode of regulating the conditions of observation transacts a brilliant exercise in organization, categorization, stratification, quantification, tabulation, and prioritization. The logic that drives his method entails efficient orderliness, systematic astuteness, and unambiguous clarity of thought. Words are sequestered and regrouped by virtue of substantial resemblances and temporal successiveness. Tradition is divided into strata or layers which are measured according to chronological gradation. A logic of quantification places high value on the numerical strength of materials. Logic also differentiates between nonessential, secondary accretions or revisions and the primary core complex. And the principal agent in ascertaining the one historical sense is the Baconian method of inductive reasoning, a branch of logic that infers from multiple particulars to indivisible singularity.

If we proceed from the assumption that Jesus was by all accounts a speaker of sayings and parabolic stories, how do his words fare under the rule of method and do they obtain justice before the bar of logic? Jesus was a speaker, not a scribe, and not even a rhetorical composer by way of dictation. All our thinking about Jesus' proclamation ought to proceed from this fact. Therefore, the historian, intent on retrieving Jesus' message, has to come face to face with the intractably difficult issue of speech. She or he will first have to learn that speech, in distinction from writing, is not traceable to external verification. Speech surrenders itself in the act of speaking. While the voicing of sayings and parables was destined to affect minds and lives of hearers, it left no externally visible traces. A text outlasts the act of writing, but oral words spend themselves in the act of speaking and live on variously in the minds of hearers. It is hard to escape the impression, therefore, that the words voiced by the historical Jesus are not available to us for purposes of classification or quantification.

Words when spoken have no quantifiable existence. Logic's critical apparatus, on the other hand, utterly depends on external linguistic visualization and on a status of permanence assumed to be intrinsic to recorded language. It

---

73. Crossan, "Historical Jesus as Risen Lord."

operates in the visual world of photographic precision, displaying clean outlines of strata and substrata, and making clinical incisions into tradition.
Logic's competence to depersonalize and reorganize knowledge grows out of
and relies on a long and intense experience with the written and printed word.
But if spoken words "cannot be 'broken' and reassembled,"[74] logic cannot take
possession of the performative poetics of Jesus' proclamation. We are bound to
conclude that the oral performance of his words is unknowable through formal thought based on literary or typographical sensibilities.

Reimagining Jesus' oral poetics is a task supremely difficult because it not
only goes against the grain of deep-seated print conventions, but it operates in
the face of a scholarship laden down with centuries of literary manners and
mannerisms. Take, for example, the issue of *the original saying*. Crossan's
methodology aside for the moment, the quest for the historical Jesus is heavily
based on the premise of the retrievability of the single, literal saying. It is widely
assumed to be an inescapably logical fact of linguistic life. But what characterizes orality is plurality of speech acts rather than *the original saying*. It is an
incontestable fact of oral life that speakers tend to restate words and retell stories in order to assure connection with hearers. This need for reiteration applies
with special force to the charismatic, itinerant speaker whose mission utterly
depended on the receptive quality of his message. Addressing the same people
frequently and different people deliberately, he would have had no choice but
to communicate his message more than once. Plurality, not single originality,
would be what distinguished his speech.

If we are going to develop sensibilities toward oral poetics with an adequate
hermeneutical propriety, we will do well to emancipate ourselves from a deeply
ingrained existential commitment to the original saying. When Jesus spoke an
aphoristic saying at one place and subsequently chose to deliver it elsewhere,
neither he nor his hearers perceived this other rendition as a *secondary* version
of the *primary*, original saying. Rather, each delivery was an autonomous
speech act. This second rendition could in fact be identical with the first rendition, or it could be at variance with it, especially if delivered before a different audience. But whether the saying was different or identical, it would not
have occurred to the speaker or his audiences to differentiate between an original and a secondary version, because each rendition was considered an original
or, to be more precise, *the* original. But when we acknowledge that *the original
saying* is pointless in orality because oral life traffics in a plurality of originals,
we have not simply moved from a singular to a plural conceptualization.

---

74. Walter J. Ong, S.J., *The Presence of the Word: Some Prolegomena for Cultural
and Religious History* (New Haven: Yale University Press, 1967), 323.

Rather, we have gained a glimpse of an oral poetics in which the very idea of *the original saying* is unintelligible.

Crossan, unlike many questers, shows some awareness of the incompatibility of *the original saying* with oral performative aesthetics. He makes a concession to oral speech by introducing the notion of "the aphoristic core," or "the *ipsissima structura.*" The mnemonically stable generic base is attributable to Jesus and its precise meaning is determined by recontextualization into the historical matrix. Now it is well known that oral performers operate with features of stability, usually referred to as *formula* or *theme.* But Crossan, unlike oral theorists, uses stability to reduce it to singular meaning: the core complex of "Kingdom and Children" is reduced to the single shocking metaphor of the acceptance of nobodies into the Kingdom of God. Admittedly, it remains a possibility that a single meaning resides in the structure of stability. But as a rule, the core structure of a saying rarely gets us to the performative realities of oral speech. In fact, nowhere is the equation of core abstraction with single meaning less suitable than in oral tradition. More often than not the aphoristic core gives us the instrument on which the music was played. And what matters in oral life is not just the instrument but very much the music the artist managed to play, and he or she performed the music by acting on the core structure, varying it, modulating it, transforming and mutating it. *Variability of core structures rather than reduction of core structure to single meaning is what typifies oral performance.* In Crossan's search for structural stability we discern one of logic's deepest desires, namely to conquer the flux of temporality and to secure time-obviating permanence. But the proclamation of the charismatic itinerant speaker is not reducible to the core structure any more than it is reducible to single meaning. It rather occurred in multiformity that was tantamount to multioriginality. A thrice-narrated parable was not comprehensible as the one authentic parabolic rendition and two variables thereof any more than it was comprehensible in terms of a core structure and three variables thereof, but only as three equiprimordial renditions.

Crossan seeks to make a concession to plural renditions by privileging majority rule. Multiple attestation is credited with historical authenticity, although, as we saw, he does not take seriously plurality as plurality because his principal objective is to downgrade the plural to the singular. But the issue of plural rendition still cuts deeper, because multiple attestation of a saying is highly plausible not only on the level of Jesus speech, but on the level of tradition itself. Crossan's own work[75] has shown convincingly that preservation of the past as past was not the only, or even most significant, driving force of tradition's collective

---

75. See esp. Crossan, *In Fragments.*

remembering. The deepest impulse driving the tradition was a rememorization of the past in the interest of the present, that is, a desire to legitimate the past as present.[76] On this view of the tradition, multiple occurrences of and variations on a saying are first and foremost evidence of the utility and popularity of that saying in the context of cultural memory. This fact neither confirms nor disconfirms Jesus' own utterance. But it is inadmissible to posit *as a matter of methodological principle* the iterative and adaptive behavior of tradition as ground for historical authenticity.

Equally problematic is the exclusion of all instances of single attestation from a reconstruction of Jesus' life. The matter weighs all the more heavily if we consider that of altogether 522 sayings and story complexes Crossan has inventoried, 342 have single attestation.[77] That is to say that approximately two-thirds of the traditions attributed to Jesus are excluded from consideration because of single attestation. It makes sense in terms of method, but little sense in terms of history. The procedure is incontestably in compliance with the logic of a quantifying methodology. We exile from consideration all that does not conform with reason's centralizing logic of identity and noncontradiction. But when one keeps in mind that we are dealing with a personality who was ill tolerated by the Jewish establishment, convicted by the Roman power structure, and whose life and death initiated a highly consequential process of rememorization, one cannot exclude a sense of poignant authenticity about this person any more than one can rule out a distinctive individuality about his speech. For this reason, the systematic excision of two-thirds of Jesus' sayings traditions on grounds of single attestation runs the risk of seriously distorting the reconstruction of his life and message. To be sure, singularity of utterance neither confirms nor disconfirms authenticity. But can it *as a matter of methodological principle* be excluded from consideration altogether?

Let us pause at this point and reflect on Crossan's project by way of analogy with an example taken from classical Greece. Let us imagine a historian of classical antiquity who has been commissioned to write the biography of, say, the pre-Socratic philosopher Heraclitus of Ephesus. Our historian proceeds by focusing on Heraclitus's 130 fragments that have come down to us and restores their original version, or rather their structural core, comparing them among themselves and with fragments preserved by later writers. Next the historian reinstates the core fragments into the context of sixth- and fifth-century Greek

---

76. See especially Jan Assmann, *Das kulturelle Gedaechtnis: Schrift, Erinnerung und politische Identitaet in fruehen Hochkulturen* (Munich: Verlag C. H. Beck, 1992), 29–86.

77. Crossan, *The Historical Jesus*, xxxiii, 434.

history to ascertain their authentic meaning in history. Can the resultant literary product based on this mode of selecting, reducing, and recasting the Heraclitus tradition come close to anything like the philosopher's historical life? The analogy is unfair, you might say, because Heraclitus was a philosopher whose sayings were meant to be abstracted from life, whereas Jesus was presumed to be a charismatic, prophetic teacher whose sayings were meant to address the human condition. In turn, one might ask whether Heraclitus' often obscure and riddling fragments were entirely unrelated to the civil catastrophe of the ruthless suppression of revolting Greek cities by the Persian king Darius I. But the real question is whether one can lay claim to the historical life of a Heraclitus, or a Jesus, or Napoleon, or George Washington, or a Madame Curie by relying exclusively on the sayings and speeches of these personages, however well their words are contextualized in their respective historical settings. Is there a single historian who has based her or his reconstruction of the life of a historical person on an extremely select group of sayings attributed to that person? In spite of Crossan's supreme confidence in method, the design of his biography based on an anthology of sayings relies on a model of historiography which, I assume, is shared by few outside the guild of biblical scholarship.

CONCLUSION

Beginnings and endings are painful, in life as in literature, and in bringing our reflections on the search for the historical Jesus to a conclusion we seek not to foreclose the debate. The five propositions that follow are intended to encourage fresh thought, for such is the status of the discourse—burdened with redundancy and institutionalized disciplinary conventions—that new voices are urgently needed.

First, a major theme throughout these lectures was that of the plural versions of the legacy of Jesus. It is difficult to deny that Jesus, speaker of aphorisms and parables, delivered similar and variable, but always equiprimordial renditions of his proclamation. If we think of Jesus as the beginning of tradition, we should think of beginning not as *the* original saying or *the* original structure of a saying, but as a plurality of similar and different versions. In the beginning were the words. As for the New Testament, far from putting forth a single model of Christ it delivers a persuasive case in favor of plural christologies. The early tradition itself is a telling testimony to rememorization, a ceaseless process of delivering Jesus' past into the present of hearers. Patristic and medieval exegesis by and large abhorred the incarceration of what were perceived to be the inexhaustible riches of the Bible into the single, literal sense. If by irony we mean achieving the reverse of what we initially intended, the modern search for the historical Jesus is fraught with irony. But it is also my conviction that the *enormity of the irony* has not fully sunk in yet in Western consciousness. One is all too often operating on the deep-rooted and indomitable premise that the quest is taking us closer and closer to the historical truth. But unless we take the long view of history, we remain unaware of what is happening. We left the house of ancient, patristic, and medieval polyvalency and in the spirit of Enlightenment aspired to the solid ground of the single sense—only to end up with the new plurality of a bewildering proliferation of seemingly interminable lives of Jesus. *Every single new life of Jesus enlarges our experience of pluralism, and takes us further away from the intended single, representational sense.* Postmodernist philosophy more resolutely than ever has sensitized us to the interminable potential in language, deferring present fulfillment in order to keep the desire in language alive. There is no escaping the plural experience. If believers are fearful of plurality in the Christian tradition and of its potentially detrimental effects on faith, let us remember that in the realm of art we have long been accustomed to plural representations—an experience that has commonly been considered inspiring rather than destructive to religious sensibilities.[78]

Second, Johnson and Crossan share a common denominator. This is the case in spite of the fact that they inhabit different intellectual worlds. Johnson's faithful embrace of the so-called biblical Christ is distinctly antithetical to Crossan's meticulous attentiveness to the historical Jesus. In fairness, Crossan is more conciliatory toward the tradition than Johnson is toward the historical Jesus. For Johnson, "Christian faith is not directed to a human construction about the past; that would be a form of idolatry."[79] Crossan on his part concedes "that there will always be divergent historical Jesuses, [and] that there will always be divergent Christs built upon them."[80] These differences apart,

---

78. On the issue of biblical pluralism see esp. Karlfried Froehlich, "'Aminadab's Chariot': The Predicament of Biblical Interpretation," *Princeton Seminary Bulletin* 18, no. 3 (1997): 262–78; see esp. p. 269: "History must give us perspective—and today we must stress the plural: perspectives, that is, insight into the various options of looking at the vast enterprise such as biblical interpretation." See also Ulrich Luz, "Kann die Bibel Heute Noch Grundlage Für die Kirche Sein? Über die Aufgabe der Exegese in einer Religioes-Pluralistischen Gesellschaft," *NTS* 44 (1998): 317–39; see esp. p. 321: "Das augustinisch-reformatorische 'sola scriptura' hat sich nicht als Grundlage der Kirche, sondern eher als ein Leitmotiv ihrer Spaltung bewiesen.... Paradoxerweise scheint das reformatorische Schriftverstaendnis seine eigene Dekonstruktion mit ausgeloest zu haben."

79. Johnson, *The Real Jesus*, 143.

Johnson and Crossan both incline toward equating truth with the intelligibility of one monolithic aspect of the tradition, be it the so-called biblical Christ or the historical Jesus. This exclusivity of emphasis has the effect of overriding plurality and/or discrediting parts of the tradition. One is reminded of the words of David Tracy, cited in an epigraph to this piece, that thought since Enlightenment "became trapped in ever narrower models of what could count as truth."[81] Johnson is aware of this when he claims that by "reducing everything to a single dimension, the historical model distorts what it can know and misses a great deal of what is important to know."[82] As we observed, Crossan denigrates Christian identities and experiences that are incompatible with the very historical profile of Jesus in which he has invested so much labor. But could not in principle a similar objection be raised in view of Johnson's project? By making a unilateral investment in the so-called biblical Christ, has he not leveled the plurality of traditions within the New Testament, altogether negated the religious significance of the historical Jesus, and misconstrued parts of the Christian tradition? Could not these flaws that are distinctive of the positions taken by Johnson and Crossan arise from their respective totalizing hermeneutics, an overemphasis on a singular aspect of the tradition at the high cost of oversimplifying Christian complexities, limiting Christian identities, and excluding Christian experiences?

Third, to the extent that we have submitted the quest to critical inquiry, we have done so not to dismiss its relevancy but rather to hold the rapture of historical positivism in check, and to replace hermeneutical complacency with hermeneutical energy. In observing "a downright astonishing optimism"[83] with which (especially in North American scholarship) the *historical quest* is undertaken, one cannot help but wonder whether we have lost all sense of the *hermeneutical quest* and its agonizing coping with otherness, a central issue in which hermeneutics and ethics converge. Sometimes it seems as if Bultmann had never coined the famous dictum that "every interpretation is necessarily sustained by a certain *prior understanding* of the subject,"[84] an insight that he

---

80. Crossan, *The Historical Jesus*, 423.

81. David Tracy, *Plurality and Ambiguity: Hermeneutics, Religion, Hope* (San Francisco: Harper and Row, 1987), 31.

82. Johnson, *The Real Jesus*, 172.

83. Jens Schröter, *Erinnerung an Jesu Worte: Studien zur Rezeption der Logienueberlieferung in Markus, Q und Thomas* (Neukirchen-Vluyn: Neukirchener Verlag, 1997), 482–83.

84. Rudolf Bultmann, "The Problem of Hermeneutics," in *Hermeneutical Inquiry*, vol. 1, ed. David E. Klemm (Atlanta: Scholars Press, 1986), 113–33; see esp. 126; German original in *ZThK* 47 (1950): 47–69.

owed both to Schleiermacher and to Heidegger. There is an understandable propensity among many authors of lives of Jesus to view their text as the authentically documented blueprint, be it for liberation, or for repudiation, or for both. But the post-Enlightenment discourse has taught us that there are no innocent authors, no innocent texts, no innocent eyes, no innocent ears, and no innocent readers. By now we should be cognizant of the authorial anxiety of influence (authors absorbing, competing with, and reading against other authors), of the instability of all texts, and of the politics of reading. That language both reveals and conceals is an insight that has spread far beyond the little mountain cabin in the Black Forest. Method, the inalienable tool of all historical research, stipulates what it will accept as evidence and stakes out a domain within which acceptable answers are expected to fall. Given these and numerous other difficulties exposed since the Enlightenment, should we not acknowledge that the aspiration to reach the underived origin—assuming that this zero level ever existed—will forever remain unsatisfied? The search for the historical Jesus betrays the force and direction of our desire, without ever assuring us a safe possession.

Fourth, we value the historical quest and we assert its signal importance, even as we relativize some of its assumptions and problematize the attainability of its final objective. When in the tradition of Kähler and Johnson it is stated that faith based on the works of history ceases to be pure faith, we in return invoke the "ethics of remembering." Traumatized by the carnage of this century, faith must not be granted immunity from "the rectitude of fact,"[85] and faith cannot be allowed ever again to remain aloof from, insensitive to, and untouched by the forces of history. But precisely in what manner ought the Christs of the gospels be sensitized to our reconstruction of Jesus, and in what manner does our reimagined Jesus of history affect the gospels' images of Christ? In the Christian tradition, the "ethics of remembering" may be informed by the Augustinian hermeneutics that aspired "an interpretation contributing to the reign of charity."[86] This does *not* mean, for example, that we eliminate, in the spirit of nineteenth-century liberal theology, Jesus' miracles because they appear to conflict with the logic of history. Miracles have long been assigned an indispensable locus in the plot construction of the narrative gospels, as we read them with a postcritical "second naiveté." But the ethics of remembering, informed by Augustinian charity, suggests that the historical Jesus may indeed serve as a measure for the gospels when the latter inflict harm

---

85. Wyschogrod, *Ethics of Remembering*, 63.
86. Saint Augustine, *On Christian Doctrine*, trans. D. W. Robertson Jr. (New York: Macmillan, 1958), book 3, sec. 15, p. 93.

upon others. When, for example, we observe how the gospels increasingly exonerate Roman authorities from Jesus' execution and correspondingly implicate the Jews, the ethics of remembering demand that we call upon history to serve as a corrective to the harm tradition has done.

Fifth, the issues of single sense versus plurality of senses, of history versus faith, and fact versus fiction cannot be the last word in these lectures. On the matter of the historical Jesus not everything conforms to these time-honored, conventional categories, and not everything submits to verbal, pictorial, or electronic mediation. We insisted on the limits of logic, and we now acknowledge the paralysis even of charity. The reason for our representational limits, we claimed, does not lie in our protective attitude toward faith, but in the trauma of facticity itself. There exists, for example, an inordinately large and exceedingly learned mass of materials on the passion narrative. Scholars have examined the death of Jesus from all possible angles: history, jurisprudence, sources, and narrative. But from the perspective of the "ethics of remembering," historical accuracy, judicial astuteness, literary sources, and even the poetics of narrative remain ignorant in the face of this death. How strange that scholars in their busyness to explore all aspects of Jesus' death rarely, if ever, have attested to the unimaginable nature of the crucifixion. Fact or fiction, history or faith, single or multiple sensibility, logic or even charity—the execution by crucifixion remains forever unrepresentable.

Index